Dedicated
to
YOU
just as you are

For Sara—
appreciating what
we share, and with
love ... WHATEVER—
Frances
Christmas Day
1981

I Want
ONE
Thing

An Autobiography

Frances Horn, Ph.D.

DeVorss & Company
P.O. Box 550
Marina del Rey, California 90291

Copyright © 1981
by Frances Horn

ISBN: 0-87516-455-2
Library of Congress Card Catalog Number: 81-67050

Printed in the United States of America
by Book Graphics, Inc., California

Contents

Introduction

by Brugh Joy, M.D.

Humanity as a whole is just beginning to realize that there are many degrees of conscious awareness or states of consciousness available to each individual. Most people assume that intelligence is the determining factor as to which degree of consciousness one may be experiencing, and that the level of intelligence fixated in a narrow range is for the life-time of an individual. Almost all psychological evaluation and theory is based on this premise.

Through very powerful experiences, i.e., confrontation with death or life-threatening disease (both often leading to the religious conversion experience), through exigent situations or through highly charged emotional crises, the awareness of individuals and the feats they are capable of performing can be vastly heightened, expanded or altered. A completely different perspective of reality may ensue. Abilities may emerge such as super-human strength, as in the case of little old ladies picking up portions of an automobile to save life. Seemingly impossible healing abilities may manifest, causing cure of incurable diseases either in the individuals themselves or in others who come into contact with heightened individuals. Sometimes abilities such as the power to see future tense and past tense become manifested. The list is a long one and I don't want to focus on specifics, but rather to offer the reader a scaffolding on which to appreciate better the importance of Frances Horn's lucid autobiography.

As you shall soon discover, Frances experienced her first expanded and sublime state of consciousness at the age of 22. To this day she is only beginning to understand how this event and others later in her life took place. I believe that this is true, despite her careful and clear presentation of the circumstances surrounding these events. It is because of Frances' attention to detail, and her honesty, that we as the readers can catch glimpses of possible mechanisms of consciousness leading to what she terms *wisdom* or *expanded states* that she as the perceiver-experiencer does not see or relate to us.

Perhaps if I go back to my opening remarks—that there are degrees of conscious awareness or states of consciousness—and establish a simple functional outline, we can more fully appreciate what Frances and more and more people are experiencing, in varying degrees, in their lives.

Ordinary awareness—that in which we ordinarily operate in our daily lives and the one in which intelligence does play a role—colors over 99% of what and how we experience ordinary life. Most people live an entire lifetime in this state, never experiencing any other possibility. They may hear about people who have had unusual experiences or unusual powers, but the vast majority of these people do not truly believe such states exist and they have no real idea of what it is like to experience life from another level of awareness.

Below (just a term I shall use; not meant to imply being

beneath ordinary awareness for, after all, where *is* awareness anyway?) is the subconscious with all its forces—emotional, sexual, instinctual, physical, etc. These are powerful forces which emerge in the ordinary awareness only at certain times under certain conditions. These forces dominate the motivations and actions of most, if not all, people in an unconscious manner. They can sometimes be called forth at will, but usually require specific stimuli to be elicited. There are levels below the subconscious, but for our purpose let's discuss another level, the superconscious.

The superconscious awareness is experienced as a sense of universality, of non-duality. It is a true Spiritual experience. In this level reside unconditional Love, resolution of conflict and enormous forces which are capable of changing the course of an individual's life and ordinary physical reality. There are levels beyond the superconscious, but again my intent is to focus on a simple structure which will suffice to give a new perspective from which to view the story of Frances.

With the sketch of the three most germane levels of awareness we must next understand that each person has potential access of varying degree and at various times to the superconscious and to the subconscious and to the forces contained within each. Dreams are the most common experience in the awareness of individuals. There are other possibilities as I shall describe. No two people experience the same degree of the superconscious nor have the exact same experience even when of the same degree. We must then appreciate that when a luminous experience occurs it usually is not durational and one has the sense of loss or contraction of consciousness as the individual re-enters ordinary awareness. This is very similar to awakening from vivid dream states occurring while sleeping. The same holds for when one enters the subconscious realms.

What does all the above have to do with Frances' autobiography? Well, with this structure one can better appreciate that when she is talking about *I Want One Thing,* this one thing is not contained in nor experienced by her or anyone else's ordinary awareness. It belongs to what we are calling the superconscious state, transcending all the distortions, confusion and prejudice of ordinary awareness. Although not specifically stated in her written presentation, we can sense the forces or energies which created the possibility for her to enter new and truly expanded states. Over and over again, Frances emphasizes the importance of the experience of the superconscious and presents her ideas of how one can achieve this state. With exceptional clarity, she dissects out the events in her life which surround each break-through. But I didn't get the sense that Frances saw the importance of the energy of crisis, chaos and conflict as the actual forces which propelled her to the superconscious realms.

Shocking, isn't it? That all the life experiences which we think are wrong or bad or guilt-producing are the very circumstances which generate an energy for change and the opportunity to enter the superconscious realm even if only briefly.

Life's struggles are necessary. We grow best under the pressure of conflict and chaos. We tend to fall asleep when life is monotonous We must have contrast to remain with even a degree of hope for vaster understanding and self-realization. And that's my very point—humanity has found, and Frances clearly displays, a very successful mechanism to create force for change of one's life. It doesn't matter what the specific event is—only the intensity of the event as perceived by the experiencing person matters. So when you read about Frances' canoe experience, look for the forces which are creating the opportunity for a superconscious experience. What she does not reveal to you is that she was actually rejecting life as she had experienced it up to the canoe experience. You will learn of the reasons when she reveals her past. But, to the point, she also had just begun to embrace the way of a newly perceived Jesus as a model on which to base her own life. In her case this predisposed her for a Spiritual Experience. Reading further we enter the canoe—Frances is 22, sexually attracted to a married man, within 24 hours of having vowed to live a Christian-like life, and whammo—the forces for crisis arise and work their magic.

We now shall be able to see that Frances Horn reveals in her autobiography more than just a very interesting and clearly presented psychological dissection of her life's experience punctuated with humor, humiliation, beauty and chaos, which is enough to cause one to enjoy reading this informative book. But because of her length of life and her mental brilliancy at age seventy-four, we get the benefit of seven and a half decades of interwoven and actual themes and patterns to understand better the importance of the good and the bad experiences in *relationship,* not as separate and isolated events. Once this is appreciated in another person, you as the reader can better appreciate your own life's opportunities when you are in crises. The chaotic mechanism which most people unconsciously use to cause change in their understanding about and experience of Life may not be appropriate in a latter developmental period; but for now, humanity—we in general—grow through crises, whether it be through disease, mental conflict or through wars—whether political, economic or Holy in nature.

How many of you have passed through difficult times—marital conflict, drug abuse, alcohol, immorality, financial crises, war, etc., only to discover a sense of maturation of mind, strength of spirit and character, and gratitude—yes, gratitude—for the experience?

I do believe there comes a time in a soul's development when the forces of conflict, fear of death, and addiction to intensity are not necessary to generate energy to lift the awareness into the superconscious level. The ego shall have served its purpose and shall fall away—atrophy so to speak. But—first things first. Most of us grow through egotistically created experiences and traumas.

Frances on first meeting is a truly radiant and loving being. It wasn't until someone exerted pressure on her—stretched her defenses and her firmly held views on reality —that she had the opportunity of resolving unconscious patterns. Who would dare emotionally slaughter a seventy-four-year-old very loving and dedicated woman whose major quest is to somehow serve humanity? In Chapter 12 you will find that I would, and did, stress Frances because I sensed her potential and I love this soul beyond even her wildest imagination.

I sense in Frances the impending development as a truly great manifesting Being, who when fully realized will make her present presence seem subtle. Because of the experiences of her life, she is stronger and more radiant. She has a deeper sense of self and Self. She is more genuinely compassionate with even more mental clarity than before. She knows she is growing and she never gives up!

What more can a book do for a person than to help point a way through life which gives to its readers insight, clarity, inspiration, and honesty—particularly honesty?

There is so much more to say about the book, Frances, and the concepts I have presented above, but let the experience begin. I suspect that you and Frances have much in common.

Brugh Joy

Lucerne Valley, California
March 30, 1981

PREFACE

Who Am I?

WHO AM I? A short-order cook in a nudist park, and a dinner guest in the palace of the Maharajah of Mysore. At one time I was a student in the gentle world of an Oxford college, and at another time I made ninety beds a day and cleaned toilets in a summer camp. I stole money from my sister's first earnings, and I learned something about unconditional love which changed the quality of life of a few people who had cancer. I was loved and cherished as a child and I carried a profound and unrecognized conviction of worthlessness and rejection. I didn't accept myself, and yet I faced the world as capable, successful, brilliant, and independent.

After experiencing an expanded level of consciousness which brought me freedom, joy, and a love without possessiveness or attachment, I spent years struggling in a constricted level of awareness and of relationships where the pain sometimes made death seem preferable. I had so desperate a need for the approval and liking of others that I almost never let them (or myself) see the hurt, fear, anger, and resentment I sometimes felt toward them. I was the ray of sunshine, and one day I grew enough to be the raging, hating, hurting fury I was feeling myself to be. On another day I knew that I was someone who included them both, and who included it all.

Seventy-four years of living have taught me a lot of things. No, not really. They have taught me one thing. I call it The Wisdom and I am writing this book to tell you what I think it is. What you do or don't do about it is your business and I'll love you either way.

But I'd like to make The Wisdom clear, because I think it is clear, and I think it is simple. Not easy, but simple. I've spent a couple of years looking for the words that would say it to you, and each of the efforts has been set aside.

Now I see that the means for telling you how I think we find self-realization and the fulfillment of our highest potential is for me to give you my own life. It will make clear what one person's life has shown as a way to balance, wholeness, inclusiveness, steadiness, joy.

Who do I think I am to be telling you that I understand clearly what The Wisdom is? And that I agree that it looks hard? And that I know that the cost is as nothing when compared with the results it brings? Well, I propose to tell you who I am, so you can answer those questions.

Living my life has given me an answer to "What is the way?" Sharing my life may serve a similar purpose for you. So I give you my life.

CHAPTER 1

The Wisdom

I THINK IT'S wonderful that you are reading this book. I wrote it for you. I don't think I could have done it unless I believed that what I would tell you could make a real difference in your life. That's your choice, of course. My part is to say clearly what I see as a way to fulfillment for each one of us and for our world, and then to offer you a chance to look at how this has worked in my life.

All through this book you will see exactly what I mean by "want one thing." You'll also see what happened to me when I did that and what happened when I didn't do it, all the way up to the present. The difference in my life—in my body, emotions, mind, spirit—is so striking that you may ask, "What did she do to make that much difference in the quality of her life at different times?"

It all goes back to our basic urge toward fulfillment and well-being. This priceless gift of our nature pushes and pulls us in the direction of the realization of our maximum potential as human beings. It doesn't let us rest, no matter how many blind alleys we try. It is an inborn impulse to relate satisfactorily to whatever reality may be. That urge will guide us to the way that brings fulfillment.

It has been prodding me for a long, long, time. When I was twenty-two years old, I actually experienced "the way that works" and I thought I knew what it meant to want one thing. My life was transformed, for a time. But it has taken another fifty years for me to understand much more about this transformational process from one level of life to another. I don't believe that everyone has to take that long. This book may help you to take less time and less pain to realize your Self. But I promise you that the results will be more than worth whatever time and pain it takes.

This whole book is about The Way—the way to experience well-being and fulfillment within ourselves and in our relationships with all that surrounds us. The way is to want one thing. We can choose to change from wanting many things, people, and happenings, to wanting one thing. As long as we want a lot of things or people or happenings, we can't be sure of getting what we want because we have little control over these outer things. And we're at the mercy of conflicting desires within ourselves. Anxiety, dissatisfaction, indecision, frustration, and despair are present or lurking around the corner if our desires are attached to specifics. And they nearly always are.

The secret, which is no secret because it has been known and taught for thousands of years by the wisest among us, is to want one thing you can always have. That way you always have what you want. Your single desire is fulfilled.

When we choose to want this one thing, we feel whole, because instead of being a battleground for sub-personalities and separate parts of ourselves, we choose a single direction, into which the energies of all the parts of ourselves can express or not, as wholeness or appropriateness dictates.

We exclude nothing in our view of What Is, and this growing sense of the oneness of all things results in our ability to feel and express an inclusive, unconditional, non-judgmental love.

In this book I'm going to describe as simply as possible what I think it means to want one thing, as a way to self-realization. Throughout human history this has been described in many different forms as part of widely varied belief systems. I'm suggesting that this way can be understood and experienced without adherence to any particular system of belief. You can try it and see what it opens up for you. Here is how I first learned about the way.

CHAPTER 2

How I Learned About Willingness

I'M GOING TO begin with the summer of 1929, when I was twenty-two years old. Two very different but closely related experiences in canoes on a remote lake in eastern Canada shaped my life as have no other happenings. In one incident I was alone. In the other I was with a married man for whom I was feeling a strong sexual desire.

That summer I was participating in a seminar which I thought might answer the question, "What do I have to do to get the most possible out of life?" Later I'll fill you in on all the happenings I'm aware of that made me ready for those moments on Island Lake. But for now, so that from the beginning you may share the meaning to me of those two experiences, it will be enough to say just this much about the setting.

I was with about thirty Canadian and American men

and women who were spending every morning, seven days a week for five weeks, answering the questions of a Canadian scholar named Dr. Henry Burton Sharman. We were supposed to find the answers to his questions by opening our minds, clearing away our conditioned preconceptions, and looking at the "evidence" from the book in front of our eyes. The book had been compiled by Dr. Sharman after years of exhaustive study and was called *Records of the Life of Jesus.*

I'll say more later about the study as a whole. For right now I'd like simply to convey to you that the whole subject was a big surprise to me, that I was astonished and delighted to see all kinds of "ideas about" Jesus disappear as apparently non-historical, and to see emerging what to me was a brand new, fresh, compelling figure. We followed the movements of a remarkable young Jew whose own deepest experiences clashed with much of his heritage. Most striking of all to me was that he kept giving the same answer, in different forms, to my question, "What do I have to do to get the most possible out of life?" His answer seemed to be, "Turn over the right to direct your own life."

This was a repugnant idea to me. I had been a very self-directed person. I had a strong sense of my own self and of my right to choose whatever I wanted to choose. The idea of renouncing that, and surrendering all of that, voluntarily, to something which I didn't even understand, seemed alien indeed. I wrestled and struggled with the concept over a period of several weeks, and each time that we encountered this central teaching in one of its varying forms, I seemed to be presented more and more irrevocably with the realization that apparently this man was saying one thing in many ways, about the means to self-realization. To achieve the level of life which he believed was available to mankind, one condition had to be met by the individual; namely, to give up what I had thought was uniquely mine as a human being: the right to want what I wanted when I wanted it. This seemed to me a very large step to take, a real surrender of what I identified as my self.

On the other hand, the inducements began to look more and more appealing and compelling. We studied carefully a number of passages in which we could see this young man interacting with his environment, and I was impressed with what he was. We made distinctions between things which probably happened as described, and things which probably did not happen as described. We concluded that some of the words almost surely had been spoken and that others almost surely had not been spoken.

Out of all this there grew up in me a powerful, impressive, deeply moving picture of a person who spoke with an amazing authority, apparently out of his own personal experience, which was at variance with many of the ideas in his culture. When I began to see what his life might really have been, I had to conclude that if I did not take seriously what he was saying, I might be losing out on a very great potential for my life.

Just here it is important for me to emphasize one vital point which was emerging from our study. The way ("lose your life") led to a result ("save it alive"). The *motivation* for consciously engaging in the transformational process was Self-fulfillment in an ultimate sense. Although the way sounded like self-destruction, it was the means to achieve a profoundly satisfying level of life in this world. The outcome was expressed as something highly desirable and attainable, as long as one met the condition for its realization.

I recall that for a few days I felt that I really understood the teaching. The apparent meaning of the paradoxical statement seemed quite clear . . . but nothing happened.

Then I came to the somewhat unhappy realization that apparently it was not enough to understand what this "transformational process" was. Somehow I was going to have to enact it in my own life, and this seemed a very big hurdle. However, it was one which I saw no way to avoid if I wanted to have a chance to experience the level of life which this man said was possible if one met the requirement.

It was because of all of this that one afternoon I paddled myself out onto the lake in a canoe, alone. When I was out of sight and sound of the camp, behind a small island, I lifted the paddle from the water and placed it in the canoe. I had a feeling that this was for me a vitally important turning point in my life but I didn't quite know how to begin. The bright sun warmed me and the only sound was the gentle lapping of the water against the canoe as it floated freely on the lake.

I knew that what I was choosing to do, as a means to an expanded, fulfilling life, was to turn over the direction of my life to something greater than I was. Even as I sat looking across to the wooded shore on the far side of the lake, I realized how little I understood about what I was giving my life *to*. The universe? God? Some ultimate purpose? An Undefined Best?

The silence brought me no further answer to my question about the object of the surrender. But what seemed perfectly clear was what I was to do in relation to it. So I began, "I haven't done conspicuously well in running my own life up to now. I am deeply impressed by what this man, Jesus, says is the way to fulfillment. Therefore, I am through trying to run my own life according to my own personal desires." Big deep breath.

I plunged on. "From now on I will be willing to do whatever is right, whatever God wants me to do, whatever is the will of God. Here I am. Tell me what I am to do and I will be willing to do anything, whatever that involves."

Then silence. I sat in the canoe and waited. Nothing happened.

I was not aware of expectations about what would happen next, but my feeling of a let-down when I got through with my surrender and commitment made me realize that I must have been hoping for a voice or a light or something extraordinary which would indicate that something or somebody was listening. In the absence of this, I decided there was nothing to do but to paddle back to shore. This I did.

The meaning of what I had done in that simple but genuine experience escaped me totally until the following night. I would have said, in fact, that this transformational process didn't work as promised, and I was ready to move on to try something else.

The next evening I found myself out on the lake again in a canoe. This time I was seated at the feet of a man who was quietly paddling us out onto the dark, still surface of the lake. I don't recall having spent any time alone with him before this, although he and his wife had been in the seminar group throughout the summer. In the middle of the lake he stopped paddling and the two of us sat in silence, under the stars.

It was then that I became aware of a very strong physical, sexual attraction to the man. I knew that when we got back to shore I wanted him to hold me in his arms and kiss me and tell me that he loved me in the way I was loving him. The urgency of the desire took hold of me with a burning intensity as I pictured myself in his arms.

Next came the realization that he was a husband, father of two children, with a wife who was then pregnant with their third child. Silently and inwardly I struggled back and forth between these two realities.

Suddenly, something inside of me said, "What was that thing you said yesterday?"

My immediate reaction was, "What has that got to do with anything?" (This was an unexpected and unwelcome interruption). "All I said yesterday was that I would do what was right. This is obviously right; this couldn't hurt anybody."

Then the voice inside of me answered, "But you said

you would be *willing* to do anything or not to do anything, in order to know what was right.''

Instantly I reacted with, ''Oh, I'm willing! I'm perfectly willing to do anything! I'm willing to have him love me or not love me.'' Without a second's hesitation, I knew that was a flat lie and that I was not willing in the slightest degree to be open to any outcome except the one I was longing for.

For a time I sat in an acute state of conflict between a powerful sexual urge on the one hand, and on the other, all sorts of shoulds and oughts and conditioned beliefs about what was morally right and what was morally wrong.

Then, as a result of the previous afternoon's experience, I moved for the first time in my life to a totally different level of consciousness from any I had ever been in before when facing a specific situation in which different parts of myself were at war. What happened in the next few moments was my first experience of trying consciously to place myself in a centered state of total willingness to go in any direction in order to know what direction was indicated for my action.

This state was completely new to me and yet, amazingly, I knew clearly and intuitively that there was only one thing I had to do. *I had to be willing to go either way.* The question of which of the alternatives might occur was of no importance, and the question about which of the alternatives might be right or wrong was of no importance. I actually did not again even raise the question of which might be right or wrong.

Instead, I knew that the one thing I had to do in order to embody the single intention I had voluntarily agreed to the day before was to put myself in a kind of neutral place, with open hands, and a true readiness to respond in WHATEVER way was indicated. I had no blueprint for this action of moving into willingness. Nothing I had ever known before could help me know how to do it. But the simple, clear, total intention of the day before—the level of consciousness in which I had wholeheartedly gathered myself together into an agreement to be willing to do WHAT-EVER any situation might call for—was in itself sufficient to tell me what had to happen within me in that moment of strong desire and attachment.

I concentrated entirely on getting to this place of *willingness*. It meant letting go of the hold on the specific outcome I had wanted, and allowing myself to open to WHATEVER outcome might be appropriate in the circumstances.

The one thing I knew I had to accomplish was to make the shift back to the new level of the day before, in which I could feel open and willing to allow WHATEVER needed to happen. I sat there until I made that shift, until I felt perfectly calm and clear and free. I was finished with the alternatives that had pulled me. *I was open to any option.* Strangely, I have no impression of having decided anything. It was as though something had simply clarified itself for me and the struggle was all over. There was nothing to decide.

I reached the place where I knew I had to be; namely, in the state of willingness to have things go either way. In that state, free of the specific pull to have the man love me, the whole situation appeared in another light. The idea of having him "in love" with me or I with him simply disappeared into thin air. The wholeness of the situation didn't call for that picture and it evaporated. It wasn't there any more. I had done all that I needed to do. It felt as if the whole episode had been clarified and I was finished with it.

If the story had ended here, it would have provided me with an invaluable experience of the way in which the single intention, established apart from any specific situation, can entirely change a problem one is wrestling with. In the state of willingness, the problem is seen in a totally new light, fully resolved. It is no longer even present as a problem. It's gone.

But on this occasion there was more to come. The man and I had been silent all of this time. I hadn't even wondered what he might be thinking and feeling. In fact, I had scarcely been aware of his presence because I was so involved with the single task I was working on in myself. Finally I said to him, "A strange thing happened to me. I wanted something very much and I gave it up."

He looked at me and replied, "The same thing happened to me."

Our hands met and I experienced a level of love which I had not known existed. It was an indescribable oneness and love. Yet miraculously, it held within it no trace, no shred of desire or attachment or possessiveness. It was indeed an "unconditional love," totally free, a love shared by two human beings who had reached it when each one, separately, in willingness, embraced wholeness.

CHAPTER 3

What Really Happened
in the Canoe?

IN LOOKING BACK upon that second canoe experience now, in order to permit it to be useful to you in whatever way may be possible, I note that when I at last spoke to the man in the canoe, the words I used were, "I wanted something very much and I gave it up." This could sound as though I hadn't done anything except to beat down a physical-sexual desire by the triumph of some moral principle which I thought "ought" to guide my conduct in this instance.

It was not that at all. I have detailed for you what went on inside of me, and it was not repression and denial of a still-lively, unfulfilled specific desire. Rather, it was an opening to be willing to allow WHATEVER represented, in that instance, the undefined best which I had the day before voluntarily chosen to embrace as a life-pattern.

The immediate problem resolved itself. The single, inclusive intention gave me a perspective from which everything looked and felt different, and the desire which had blocked my view of the total situation disappeared. I felt free and comfortable in the situation as it was. This would all have been true even if the second part of the story had not taken place.

We might speculate on what could have happened if the man's response had been quite different. Having let go and been willing . . . WHATEVER, I would have been sitting there in this peaceful, free state (although actually without any idea of where I really was!) and I would have been reporting to the man that I had wanted something very much and had given it up. Suppose he had replied casually, "That's interesting. So what else is new?"

What I know is that the state of consciousness I reached did not come because of the response from the man. The new level I reached was the result of the generalized intention, and the *being willing* to let go of the strong specific desire, with the resultant experience of freedom and insight that this brought. Granted, the experience of the mutually-felt non-possessive unconditional love was like a miracle. But with it or without it I had been consciously launched on my transformational journey, and sooner or later there would have grown in me an awareness of the infinitely expandable meaning of "finding your life" as a consequence of "losing it" in this way.

The two canoe experiences, taken together, created a realization that something radically new and different had happened to me. I became aware that I had entered another world, another way of being, another dimension of consciousness. The newness, freshness, and surprise of the state I woke up in made me understand why people use such extreme descriptions as "being born again." I felt like that. I was in a new world and felt like a different person.

I found that the single intention, with the willingness, affected everything in my life—my perceptions, feelings, thoughts, judgments, decisions, spontaneous actions, relationships, moods, physical well-being, ideas, plans—everything. It all began to flow from a new integrating center.

The particular example of my experience with the man in the canoe has no importance in itself. It could have involved a more trivial conflict or it could have involved a life and death decision. The example is significant only because for me it was the first conscious use of the newly centered Self, following a reorientation of my will. It was the first *Doing* after the decisive moment of *Being* in an entirely new way, the day before.

It was the first action which flowed spontaneously from the integrated Self, as I removed an emotional obstruction, not by dealing with it directly as a problem, not by repressing it, but by opening to allow the issuance of WHATEVER was appropriate in the circumstances as a whole. The generalized willingness eliminated any need for will-power or effort to deal with the specific problem.

As a friend recently said to me, "The beginning doesn't have to be a 'big deal'. You can make the commitment as best you can, and then use the next example that turns up in your life to see how it works. The specific which confronts you doesn't have to be an earth-shattering choice. It has only to be the next living moment in which a response is called for. And you know that the specific thing you are involved with doesn't matter. What matters is your state of willingness."

CHAPTER 4

Interlude

THE CANOE EXPERIENCES had left me a changed person with the feeling of awakening in another reality. Nothing had prepared me for what I was experiencing, and I walked on air. I felt at the time that I had made an all-or-nothing, once-and-for-all commitment to something greater than I was, which would reveal itself to me as "what was right."

Having made this choice to follow an undefined good to which I had voluntarily surrendered myself in the abstract, in general, and in advance, my conclusion then was that I had done this for all time and now had only to let this one choice flow into the specifics. I knew how the "total surrender" with its resultant state of willingness had dissolved the problem concerning the man in the canoe and I assumed that the struggle was now over and that life would be just an effortless moving into WHATEVER was right or best

15

in the moment. There was no way to know then that fifty years later I would still be living through one of my hardest but most fruitful struggles.

However, the experience at that time was valid. I had chosen to "let go of everything" and found myself the recipient of what felt like "more than everything" in an expanded and wondrous dimension of reality.

I thought I had given "all that I had" in choosing a single, more vast direction for my life. And that opening of the hands and of the heart in a willingness to do WHATEVER was "right," no matter what that might call for, was effective. I felt wholehearted, without conflict or inner division, free, with a joy and peace and zest I had never known. My open heart expanded in new depths of love.

But in spite of the undeniable importance of the inner change when I was at the new level of consciousness, I was not always or automatically there. It became apparent that for "all that I am" to have a single direction, without attachment to specifics, would take a long time and would be a slow task of unfolding. I had to learn much more about what that "I am" included, and to embrace it *all*.

Yes, it is true that to be open, free, non-attached, allowing the expression of wholeness . . . WHATEVER, felt to me at the beginning like being a new person; it felt like the difference between death and life. And it *was* that different when I was in the new state. What I learned slowly and painfully was that this was a level of consciousness that one enters and leaves, enters again and leaves again, apparently endlessly.

It is only recently that I have been able to look at several decades in the middle of my life with acceptance, discerning their essential contribution to the whole of my life. That period, including much of the thirty years of my marriage, had seemed almost hopelessly "off the track" and destructive. I have asked myself how I could have moved during those years to a level of life which seemed so alien to the one I was aware of in my early twenties.

I see now that part of the answer lies in my very early years. A basic pattern was laid down so deeply that it has continued to be subtly present, essentially unresolved. During the last couple of years I have been brutally confronted with it once again. This time the encounter was so painful that I mobilized the energy for resolution, and took a further giant step in my growth toward balance, stability, and well-being.

So I will tell you now about that early pattern, which many of us experience until we recognize who and what we really are. And I will tell you about the difficult middle years which led into this present period of productivity, curiosity, and feeling of oneness with the whole, WHATEVER that may be.

CHAPTER 5

The Early Pattern

WHEN I WAS a little girl my family had some jokes which must have seemed very funny to them because I heard them time and again, whenever there was a new audience. My parents' first child was a daughter, Harriet, and the family spent the next five years hoping for the arrival of her baby brother. And I arrived! As a small child I recall hearing an aunt say sympathetically, before Christmas, "Poor Gus! He would just love to buy his son an electric train that he himself could play with, but instead he has to buy Frances a doll!" And I thought, "Oh dear, look what I'm doing to my father that he can't have an electric train to play with."

Another version of this theme which recurred with painful frequency was the one about the docking of the trans-Pacific liner. A sister of my mother's was returning from the Philippines just after my birth, and since the voyage took thirty days and there was no such thing as radio, she was still anxiously awaiting the news of the long-expected baby. So, all the family was on the pier in San Francisco to greet her, along with a swarming crowd on land and all the passengers on deck. A young uncle of mine stood on the end of the pier, cupped his hands like a megaphone and yelled, "It's a girl!"

The listeners to this tale, which was often related with relish by my father, would then all but roll on the floor with laughter. And I would inwardly die a thousand deaths, feeling that it had been trumpeted to the whole world that I was not the long-awaited boy.

It has taken me a long time to realize that the words "It's a girl" were neutral and not, as I assumed, the public admission of a terrible catastrophe and the dashing of long-held hopes. So far as the people at the dock knew, this might have been the greatest possible news, after three sets of twin boys! But my value judgment was that I had been a great big disappointment to my family.

This was strange too, because I was a dearly loved and appreciated child, and I really knew that, most of the time. But the sting of that story eroded and at times wiped out my own self-acceptance in a way that has been like a thread throughout my whole life, including the devastating experiences of last year. I am remembering that the psychologist Fritz Kunkel used to say, "The first incidents we remember are the pattern we will be working on in this life." This pattern of profound non-self-acceptance masked by surface success and competence, has been mine.

In my late forties, when I was in psychoanalysis, the memories of these incidents surfaced and my analyst pointed out, "You wouldn't have amounted to anything, probably, if you'd been a boy, but as a girl you had to prove that you were better than any boy they could have had." And that really feels true. I was always "busting my gut" to achieve and to be first. I was bright and quick and I could devise ways to avoid many of the situations in which I could not excel. Outwardly I gave the impression of being self-confident, capable, popular, gifted—a "born leader." Inwardly and unawarely I lived with a profound sense of inadequacy and low self-esteem.

Another searing childhood memory burned into me a sense of worthlessness. I had just been skipped into the fourth grade and the class was learning a poem. I quickly memorized it and the teacher then asked me to help her "hear" some of the other children when they were ready to pass the memory test. A short time later as I was listening to a boy who was reciting the poem to me, he hesitated and I prompted him and he went on to finish. The teacher, who overheard this, swooped down upon us, ordered the boy to his seat and delivered a tirade at me.

She seemed out of control as she spat out the words, "You are a cheat and a liar. What you have done is unpardonable." With a sweeping gesture toward her ample bosom she intoned, "To thine own self be true." I felt that I must be too wicked to understand the meaning of the words.

I tried to protest that I had not known that I must not prompt the boy, but she swept this away. She then told me that when I went home for lunch I must tell my mother the dreadful thing I had done, and must then report back to her my mother's reception of the news.

I dragged myself home at noon, and sat in miserable silence at the lunch table where my mother and sister were chatting cheerfully. Finally I blurted out, "This morning Miss Johnson had me listen to Peter Roberts repeat his poem and I prompted him."

My mother and sister went on with their conversation. I grew desperate. What could I tell Miss Johnson about my mother's reaction?

I plunged on. "I didn't know that I wasn't supposed to prompt him." Still no response from my mother.

I trudged back to school and Miss Johnson asked, "Did you tell your mother the dishonest thing you did this morning?"

"Yes."

"What did she say?"

"She didn't say anything."

"Then you must not have told her what a wicked thing you did."

An interesting sequel to this story was that Miss Johnson also taught us arithmetic, and was introducing us to the multiplication table. Although I normally could memorize easily, I could not learn the multiplication table under her direction, try as I might. Day after day, as the other children passed the test 100% and were allowed to read library books of their choice, I took the test over and over again until at last I passed it. Since those "shameful" days, mathematics in any form has been a nemesis for me.

This reminds me of another of the stories my father liked to tell about my childhood. He sympathized with my difficulty with arithmetic because he liked to do lengthy multiplication problems in his head for the fun of it. One day when he came home and found me laboring over my arithmetic book, he said, "Today a salesman came into the office with something new. It's a machine that adds and subtracts and multiplies and divides, and if you make a mistake it rings a bell."

I put my book down and stared at him in disbelief. "Do you mean to say that there's a machine that can add, subtract, multiply, and divide, and if you make a mistake it rings a bell?" He nodded. Whereupon I picked up the arithmetic book in a gesture of complete liberation and flung it into the air over my shoulder.

As I recall that moment, I realize that a part of me has always loved the idea of something more, something new, more expanded, with the possibility of a richer experience than I have yet had. I believe we all have this, and that it is this in us which keeps us moving and seeking and trying and getting knocked down and picking ourselves up again. It expresses in the whole evolutionary process. In the deepest sense, it motivates our journey back to Source, to a recognition of the Wholeness of which we are a part.

When I was eleven, a nearly fatal accident left me with a fractured skull, nose, and some ribs. At the end of a day's picnic, a group of my sister's friends and I were straggling along a dirt road in the country when we encountered two horse-drawn gravel wagons which, fortunately for me, had just emptied their contents. The wagons moved slowly, one connected to the other by a four-by-four pole. Three of the older girls jumped onto the pole for a ride. Imitating them I also got on the pole but then reached out to pull up another girl who was trying to get on. I lost my balance and fell over backwards to the ground.

The first huge wheel of the second wagon ran over my middle. Those watching in horror said that I twisted around to try to avoid the second wheel, which lightly struck and glanced off my forehead and nose. I jumped up, my forehead streaming with blood, and the shock was so complete that I felt no pain in my head and was totally conscious and alert, aware only of pain in my side when my breathing moved the broken ribs. I was particularly elated when I was being driven to the emergency hospital in a flashy red Stutz convertible.

My mother was sent for, and because she was a trained nurse she was allowed in the operating room as the doctor tried to clean me up, and took some thirty-five stitches in my head and over and under my eye. It was not known then whether my vision would be impaired.

All of this time I chatted with my mother and the doctor, and felt no pain as he scrubbed and stitched my face. This was the Thursday before the opening of school in the autumn and I asked the doctor if I would be able to start school on Monday. He gave me some kind of answer which apparently satisfied me. This was long before the days of antibiotics.

Privately, the doctor said later to my mother that, although he had used antiseptics on my skull with a scrubbing brush to remove the ground-in dirt, there was no possible way to avoid widespread infection from which I could not possibly recover. He had therefore stitched me up only to "make a decent-looking corpse." Unaware of this, I lay in the ambulance on the way to the hospital near our home, now more comfortable with my ribs strapped up, and asked my mother to report on all that she was seeing of interest out of the window.

I must have been a sturdily built child, because although the wounds became seriously infected, I survived, and with energy to spare. My most painful recollection is of a period when I was finally home from the hospital, but the efforts to combat the infection had to continue. Our family physician was a kindly, rotund man who came each day with the unhappy task of causing me intense pain in a determined effort to save my life. He had a hypodermic needle with a huge, coarse needle. He stood over me and I had the impression that it took all of his force to jab this great thing under my eye and draw off a quantity of thick pus. I knew how he hated to do it and how it hurt him, and I knew he had to do it. I was always praised for being a brave girl, and I suppose that helped.

My mother, who nursed me devotedly through this whole thing, remarked to me several times in later years, "You must have been spared for something!" It was her acknowledgement that my survival seemed miraculous, and she sometimes said it with awe and sometimes with exasperation when actions of mine had tried her patience to the limit. But I know that my parents thought I was wonderful, when they weren't saying plaintively, "Why can't you be a little lady, like Harriet?"

It was several weeks after the accident before I got back

to school. My forehead was still bandaged and I was able to be something of a heroine as I allowed some of my friends to lift up the gauze pad and see the small hole that was still unhealed in the middle of the scar. Perhaps because I was eleven and not older, I was not then burdened by the fear of how all this would affect my looks. I think this came when, after plastic surgery, there was still some scarring and facial imbalance.

The pangs of adolescence didn't really start until after I had graduated from the eighth grade of the grammar school I attended in Alameda. Until then the boy-girl differentiation wasn't very apparent. I don't recall our ever having a school dance, although we may have had a few lessons in dancing.

A vivid memory of rejection and nonacceptability comes back from a day when I was thirteen, and the family had moved to Berkeley so that my sister could attend the University of California. I had just graduated from the eighth grade and my class had gone on to Alameda High School. One Friday afternoon early in the fall there was to be a dance in their gym and I went to it. Most of the boys and girls were strangers to me except for those from my old grammar school. Around the wall of the big bare gymnasium a row of hard folding chairs had been placed and I was sitting on one of these between the two girls who had been my best friends.

I'm really there as I bring back the memory.

The music starts and the boys begin to wander over to where the girls are sitting around the edge. A boy comes up and asks Marion to dance. She smiles at him, gets up and leaves me. Another boy approaches Helen, who murmurs something to me and goes off with the boy. I sit alone in the empty space, being a wall-flower.

I feel terrible; I want to run away and hide. Why did I ever come back? If only I hadn't come here!

When people come near I pretend to be very busy and unavailable as if I were waiting for my partner who has gone over to the other side of the room. I peer over there pretending to see him. I cannot face the fact that no one is asking me to dance. I cannot bear it; I am sure that everyone is looking at me and realizing that no one wants to dance with me. It feels like total rejection and everybody can see it happening.

How can I stand it to go on sitting here? Can I just run away and go home? It hurts so badly. It hurts so badly. I will never let myself get into a box like this again, never. I will find some other way because I cannot bear this humiliation.

In the meantime, I'll fool them by looking very much occupied. No one is to dream that I want to dance. Obviously I am so involved and busy that no one would consider asking me to dance. It is unthinkable that I should sit here allowing my actions to say "No one is dancing with me just now and I would love to dance." I cannot risk that terrible moment of allowing myself to sit quietly, open, ready and willing to dance and looking welcomingly at any prospective partner who is looking for someone to dance with. That is the *last* thing I can do. That would make me horribly, intolerably vulnerable to more hurt, more rejection.

I'll show them. They are not rejecting me because I am rejecting them first. See! Look at me—I am perfectly happy, having a wonderful time. See how I smile? I am independent; I don't need anybody. I am managing just fine, thank you. Isn't it a great party?

Years later when my husband and I were doing a lot of dancing, I sometimes thought of that "terrible" afternoon. And, at the later time, I loved the feeling of security which allowed me to sit, tacitly admitting that up to that moment no one had asked me to dance and that I was available, looking expectantly at a man who approached me, with a readiness to dance if I were asked, or to sit comfortably during that dance if I were not.

I will do my very best to explain how I think all of the

changes have come about, because the really important question for any of us is the question of "How To" and its answer. How do we find self-fulfillment, inner freedom, and the realization of our highest potential? I think the answer is to Want One Thing, and I believe that the telling of this life-story is my way to approach it with you.

About a year after the Alameda High School dance episode, where I so fiercely claimed independence and competence to mask my anguish, I was once again in a hospital. This time it was no emergency but a planned plastic surgery to try to correct some of the results of the accident three years before. A few days after the surgery I was taken in a wheel chair up to a solarium on the top floor, where other patients in wheel chairs were also enjoying the sunshine. It was a pleasant change from my room and I watched everything with interest. The shadows began to lengthen as the afternoon wore on, and one by one nurses came to claim their patients and take them to their rooms before supper.

Each time this happened I felt more uneasy. I tried to look brave and resourceful and capable, but as each patient was wheeled away I felt more anxious and helpless, a little girl in a wheel chair with a bandaged head and face, shaky and uncertain about what to do if the last person left and she was all alone, forgotten. Finally, when the last nurse came to get the last patient, I put on a brave front, although I was close to tears as I managed to say as lightly as I could, "Would you mind calling the second floor nurses to see if they have forgotten me?" A nurse finally came for me, remarking defensively, "Somebody would probably have noticed if you weren't in your room for your supper tray."

This was a kind of vulnerability and dependency that terrified me and I looked for ways to avoid it. I tried to find a niche where I could feel secure and could "succeed."

A new friend at Berkeley High School introduced me to a group she belonged to, called the Girl Reserves. Today it would be the equivalent of the "Y-Teens," the teen-age group in the YWCA. I took to it like a duck to water. I loved it and thrived in it. I could be a success and a leader. My outer sense of self-confidence bloomed into formidable proportions, although I was usually clever enough not to seem so objectionably successful as to alienate me from my "followers." My manipulations were subtle enough so that people were unaware of how much power I was using. And so was I.

One day in a group discussion, each girl was giving her comments on one line of a series of statements about conduct, one of which was, "I would be humble for I know my weakness." The girl who had that line made some sensible remarks about how she should be humble because in relation to all that was greater than she was, she was just a small, weak person with limited abilities. I was astounded by her interpretation, and burst out in honest amazement, "I had no idea that that's what that line meant. I thought it meant, 'I would be humble because I know that not being humble is my weakness.' "

A special feature for me of the Girl Reserve experience was that it offered an inspirational, spiritual element which I found agreeable. My own "religious education" had been minimal or absent, and I flourished in the non-denominational, inspirational aspects of the program, which opened some doors to an expanded awareness.

At about this time, when I was fifteen, my mother was found to have a massive brain tumor. For some three years before this she had experienced occasional terrifying convulsions after which she would be unconscious for long periods. Upon regaining consciousness she would be unable to speak for hours, although she clearly knew what she wanted to say. My father took her to whatever medical resources the San Francisco bay area offered, but no physician could determine a cause or was able to help.

It was during this trying time that my grandmother announced to me that undoubtedly I had caused my mother's illness by all the anxiety and grief I had created by my accident. This was a fairly heavy load for a youngster to bear, and I had no means to refute it. I certainly recognized that I had put my mother through a very difficult time. But now under my grandmother's pronouncement I had to internalize for a couple of years a tremendous amount of guilt, which I discussed with no one.

Finally a neurologist referred my parents to a brain surgeon who was then about thirty-eight years of age. He said that as soon as my mother walked into his office he knew that she had a tumor on the left side of her brain because she dragged her right foot slightly. In going over her history it appeared to him that the tumor had been a very long time in developing, and that quite probably the origin was in an accident she had had as a child, in which a sharp, heavy blow to the head had caused a concussion. This obviously was for me a helpful rebuttal to my grandmother's accusation, but I had probably been forced to consider deeply the inter-relatedness of events, and my part in them.

The art and science of brain surgery was still in its infancy and the prognosis was poor. The surgeon said that my mother had about one chance in ten. Two very long operations were performed, a week apart. After the second, the surgeon told my father that the tumor was benign but was so large and the hemorrhaging so great that he had not been able to remove it all. A third lengthy operation would be necessary in a few months when my mother's strength was built up sufficiently to attempt it.

When she and my sister and I were told of this, and of the very small chance of a successful outcome, a new atmosphere came about in the family. We had to face the possibility that in about three months my mother might be dead. I "grew up" during that summer. My sister was in nurses' training in San Francisco and so mother and I were alone during the day, as she tried to teach me things about cooking and housekeeping, and as she reminded me of things my father particularly liked. I think we never actually spoke of her possible death but it was implicit in everything we said and did.

Facing death in this way moved my mother to a more focused interest in spiritual things. I recall that she began to do some reading of the Psalms and of the New Testament, and she attended a Congregational Church in the neighborhood which she decided she would like to join. My father, who was as gentle and kind a man as one would ever find, felt uneasy with any institutional religion, and so he did not join in this. However, I said that I would join the Congregational Church with my mother. We had a talk with the minister, joined that church and continued to attend. All that summer I recall praying fervently that my mother would survive the operation, and not die.

I don't recall clearly the feelings which moved me into this quite serious, devoted action of joining the church with my mother. All of it was focused on the appalling possibility—even probability—that she was going to die. We were both reaching out for some kind of support and sustenance with which to face what was happening. I recall no theological questions such as: What kind of God would allow this? Or, What kind of God would intercede to reverse a probable action? I guess that what we sought and found was the simple, profound comfort of words like those in the twenty-third Psalm, "The Lord is my Shepherd, I shall not want." Some deepening and expansion of consciousness came about for me in those months.

At last the day came for the surgery to be performed, like the others, in San Francisco at the University of California Hospital. My father and I paced around for four hours, looking unseeingly at museum exhibits in a nearby building or walking the streets. From time to time we went to the surgery floor to learn thankfully that the operation was still going on. This meant, "At least she is still alive." Finally, we saw through the open doors an empty room, and quantities of blood.

We went to her room on another floor at the end of a long hall, and waited outside her door for the surgeon to come. All that he had to tell us was expressed in his bearing as he came striding toward us, his long legs seeming to carry him triumphantly as he smiled broadly. We didn't even need to hear his words, "It all went perfectly."

Mother made a rapid recovery and was able to cope with the next blow which hit the family the following year. I was sixteen, a senior in high school, when our home was completely destroyed in a fire which consumed six hundred houses in Berkeley on one hot, fiercely windy September afternoon in 1923. Mother had time only to carry out a few armfuls of things and all the rest was burned.

The fire burned down the hill to a point several blocks below our house, so that neither my father nor I ever got home. Each of us found the way to my best friend's house, where her family was packed and ready to leave. We all waited, and watched anxiously for my mother to appear, wondering how she would weather the strain of all that was happening. At last she came walking towards us, smiling cheerfully and saying to me, "The only hair you have is on your head!"

The joke about that was that, on the day before, I had joined the parade of girls who were beginning to wear "bobbed" hair, and had had my hair cut, carrying home with me a shoe-box full of long hair which had now gone up in smoke.

Strangely enough, the adjustment to the fire was surprisingly easy, partly because so many others were sharing the experience and this lent a measure of support from one another and from the community. My parents and I crowded into my grandmother's flat in San Francisco, and I commuted "backwards" across the bay to Berkeley High School to complete my senior year the following June, after which we moved back to a rented house in Berkeley.

It has been in writing these last sections that I have looked more deeply at the absence of a tragic sense of loss in the fire. The "loss" was complete enough, goodness knows. It is quite an experience, on the day after a spectacular occurrence in which a whole hillside is ablaze and only hundreds of chimneys remain standing above the embers, to walk into a store and buy a toothbrush and an undershirt. Almost everything had to be replaced. In fact, for years afterward we might find ourselves fruitlessly searching for some possession only to remember, "Oh, of course! That was before the fire."

The only books we saved were those which people had borrowed from us, and the small Hudson edition of Shakespeare, one of which my father always carried in his pocket for the daily commute to the city.

However, there was never a crippling sense of loss. Quite possibly that was because of what had happened to our values the year before when we faced the probability of my mother's death. Next to that, the possessions took their place in a wider perspective.

I appreciated this experience forty-five years later when I faced the loss of most of my physical possessions, and the death of my husband. By this time I had begun to discover a whole new conception of the meaning of "loss." From my present perspective I know that loss in the sense in which I used to experience it is now meaningless. The meaning has emerged at another level, which is beyond loss, when I am able to be beyond attachment.

During college at the University of California, I found a place in which I could be a star with an ever-widening stage. One of the campus activities was the student YWCA, a liberal group with national and international affiliations. I made my way up that ladder and became chairman of the western region and then of the National Student Council, representing student associations in hundreds of colleges throughout the country. In that connection, after having conducted a series of important meetings in New York (in my then characteristically brilliant fashion!), I returned to Berkeley to start my senior year, five weeks late. True to the pressure of my hidden rigid rule that "Frances Warnecke cannot fail," I did the impossible against great odds in the remaining weeks and almost killed myself, literally. After facing the very unusual schedule of six three-hour final examinations in the first three days (the sixth one being psychological statistics!), I collapsed with a near-fatal strep throat. Once again there were no antibiotics, and after some days I heard the doctor tell my mother that he thought I was out of the woods. But I developed pernicious anemia and was effectively flattened for months. I missed the last semester of my senior year and could not graduate with my class.

As I lay on a couch listening to music and looking out of the window that spring, I was forced to do some reshuffling of my values, and the quiet time was not wasted. For years I had been goal-oriented; I had "busted a gut" to achieve, and to prove how capable I was. I had used will-power and a bright mind to push things through in the way I wanted them to go.

During the same period I had begun to expand my awareness somewhat, and to see myself in a little perspective relative to "the universe." My father took a lively interest in astronomy and would come home from astronomical meetings with a series of stupefying statistics about distances measured in vast numbers of light years. My poor mother would hold her head and say, "Oh, Gus, don't tell me those things! They make me feel so small and helpless." But I relished them, and wrote them in my college notebook and brooded over them from time to time with appreciation and an expanded consciousness.

However, if the crunch came between an inspiring view of the infinite and a practical chance for Frances Warnecke to bowl people over with her abilities, the infinite took a back seat. And it was my need to "prove" myself, (really to myself) in the pattern of needing to overcome the "It's a girl" experience, that had all but killed me with the strep throat. All these things moved in and out of my mind that spring of 1928 when my class was getting ready to graduate and I was resting on a couch, watching the flowers grow.

Then in May I was asked to be one of six people, three men and three women, to go from the United States to an international student meeting in India in the fall. The doctor said that if I got my red blood count up I could go. That summer I had a very easy job at a primitive sort of resort in the high mountains where I could take sun baths and build up my strength. The setting was ideal, on a small lake, and I had much time to myself. This was the period in which I did my first concentrated study of Eastern religions, as a preparation for a number of months in India, Burma, China, and Japan. The meeting I would be attending was the World Student Christian Federation (student YMCA and YWCA in the American colleges) but there was a strong emphasis on the religious traditions of the countries in which we would be staying. My sustained appreciation of Hinduism, Buddhism, and Taoism began at that time.

Shortly before I was to leave for Europe on the first segment of the trip around the world, one of the staff members of the student YWCA at Berkeley, who had lived for some years in China, said to me, "Frances, when you are in the Orient I think you are going to find that superficial cleverness will not be enough. The people you will meet will see through that because they know the meaning of real wisdom." I was angry and resentful at what I sensed as her critical tone, but I pretended not to be. However, her words stayed with me and came back to me as truth during the journey. In particular, I recall an instance in China when I was giving a talk which had to be translated. I became painfully aware that personality-level charm and charisma fell flat in translation, and that only solid, honest communication reached such an audience.

As I look back now at the young woman I was in 1928, I am struck by the contrasts between parts of myself which were so different, out of touch with one another, and so unconscious. I see the bright, capable, independent leader who can and does manage and manipulate groups of people to suit her goals, who needs to be first and who selects people and circumstances where she can be first. And I see the little girl, unsure of herself, unacceptable to herself, perilously dependent on the opinion of others for self-validation. I see a young woman, sophisticated and naive, worldly and unworldly, facing outward and facing inward.

It is as this twenty-one-year-old collection of sub-personalities that, in the early autumn of 1928, I started on an eight months' trip around the world, a journey that permanently shook up my conditioned views of human customs, cultures, peoples and ideas.

CHAPTER 6

The Journey Around the World
1928–1929

IT BEGAN WITH England. Coming down the gangplank
when the ship landed at Plymouth, I managed to set my
right foot first on the shores of England, with a sense of
coming home. My maternal grandfather had come from
England and members of the family were still there, and I
would visit them later. Also, although I was in a "foreign"
country, at least the language would be the same.

Ha ha ha!!! That was the first jolt, the flow of words
sounding so strange and different to my ears, sometimes to
the point of being unintelligible. And then to be informed
that it was I who had the "accent"! Until then my manner
of speaking had been a fixed center, like a pre-Copernican
earth. Surely only other people had accents, not me. . . .
Reality began to feel slightly more relative.

And the differences in the terms they used for things!
The elevator was a lift, the trunk of a car the boot, the

hood a bonnet, a trailer a caravan, the mail the post, the line the queue, a cookie a biscuit, a cracker a biscuit, a biscuit a scone, a can a tin. I marveled that we could communicate at all.

Another striking difference which touched me deeply was the *age* of things. Coming from the last outpost of the New World on the shores of the Pacific Ocean where we were proud of our few relics of Spanish presence in the late eighteenth century, I was flabbergasted in the presence of a tiny Norman church or an even older Saxon wall and window. And evidences of all the centuries between then and now were everywhere. Subtly my realization of "Who am I?" was affected by seeing myself in relationship to this longer span of time. The perspective was beginning to be widened.

The next jolt came when I encountered the French language "as she is spoke." School records would show that I had "taken" three years of French in high school and two in college. The fact was that the teachers were American, and that we read and learned some rules of grammar, but that we almost never heard French spoken "as she is spoke" and almost never opened our mouths to speak French. No one had even thought of such a thing as a cassette tape player or a language laboratory at that point in history.

By the time I crossed the English Channel to France, I had joined the two other American women who were to be my traveling companions. They were a black woman, Juliette Derricotte, and a white woman, Erma Appleby. We were to meet our three American men counterparts in Geneva, along with the Europeans who would sail with us from Marseille to Bombay, through the Suez Canal and the Red Sea.

So, here I am now in Paris, trying to act as interpreter and travel guide to Juliette and Erma, because I "speak

French." The taxi driver is able to deposit us at an international student residence in the Latin Quarter (probably because the words were printed on a paper and he could read them). We struggle to unload our luggage on the pavement and I dig into my purse for the fare. Then I decide on the proper amount for the tip and hand it to the driver. He explodes in a torrent of abuse, waving his arms and screaming obvious curses. Then in a final dramatic gesture, he flings my coin into the gutter. . . . So much for the French tour guide.

India overwhelmed me so forcibly that to this day I have not been able to go back, although, from my present perspective, I am feeling almost ready to experience it again. The year was 1928 and I was a naive twenty-one-year-old, an idealistic yet pragmatic American who believed in sensible, efficient ways to solve problems. I took for granted a certain standard of living that gave high priority to cleanliness, health and "adequacy" of food, clothing and shelter —a standard which placed far more emphasis on plumbing than on the state of the soul.

During the months of studying before the trip, I had tried to open my mind to the assumptions which underlay much of Indian religious thought about the relative values of the "real and the unreal," about "truth and illusion," but obviously I had failed totally. I can still feel the shock as I watched sacred, skin-and-bones cows hold up traffic on the streets or wander up the imposing steps of a British bank, or as I saw the open sores on a child's eye swarming with flies.

At Benares, sacred city on the Ganges, the travel-stained pilgrims suffering ailments walked into an open-air tank in which they bathed among the rotting flowers offered by previous pilgrims. It was this water which they placed in bottles to take home to those too ill to come to the shrine.

And on the river bank, I recoiled as I watched the burning ghats where a dead body would be mostly consumed on a pile of wood but when the wood was gone, all that remained, including some parts of the body, would be shoved into the river to make room for the next one. And a few feet farther downstream, a pilgrim washing himself in the sacred river pushes aside a human arm floating by, and cups his hands to drink the sacred water.

All of this was almost too much for me. I struggled conscientiously to appreciate other elements of this great and ancient culture, but with my conditioning, it was very hard. One day a couple of us were taken by a young Indian woman to a tiny village of a dozen or so mud huts out in the country north of Calcutta. Toward the end there was not even a road or track, and we moved in small wooden boats, like hollowed out logs, up a canal. The villagers subsisted on the returns from their crop of jute, a plant which they cut and placed in ponds to rot, after which the fibers could be pulled apart to make a variety of jute products, such as rope.

Each hut had its own pond which also held fish. The men stood waist-high in the pond of rotting jute pulling the fibers apart. Then the fish died and they rotted too, and then the flesh on the men's legs began to rot into open sores. All of this time they were pulling the jute apart to prepare it for market. Each family's pond provided the place to do the family washing, the place to bathe, and the place to drink.

In my horror I cried out to our young guide, "But why don't they all get together and have some ponds for the jute and some for fish and some for washing and some to drink?" The answer as nearly as I could grasp it, and I tried hard, was that certain deeply-held beliefs made that impossible. It seemed to be a part of a religious system which I could not comprehend, but which had rules of iron.

Of course the same thing was true of the caste-system

which I had made a valiant effort to comprehend before arriving. The "sweepers," whose task was to remove the excrement, human and animal, could defile a person who was touched even by their shadow.

I was feeling overwhelmed by India and I could see that what felt unbearable to me was the *magnitude* of all the problems of hunger, poverty, disease, ignorance, superstition. I felt helpless in the face of problems which my Western mind said were intolerable for people to suffer, and for which there surely must be "practical" solutions. I was having only a beginning glimpse of the importance of beliefs and of relative value systems.

We discussed these things with the many Indian students whom we met. This was the winter of 1928-29, and the burning issue was independence for India. We were to have spent several days at Gandhi's ashram, but a mechanical problem with our ship had delayed our arrival in Bombay, and made this impossible. Gandhi's campaign of nonviolent resistance had borne fruit, and while we were there a royal commission from England was making investigations and recommendations which led finally to independence. When we asked Indian students how they would solve the problems which looked so staggering to us, they said that all would be different when the British left. "There may still be a mess but it will be our own mess." This seemed sufficient answer for them under the circumstances.

As in most other countries, a gulf existed between the lives of the very poor and those of the very rich. Our international student conference which preceded an all-India student Conference (India, Burma and Ceylon, for the first time) was hosted by the Maharajah of Mysore, who had had comfortable temporary quarters set up for us. One evening our group of a hundred or more was entertained at the palace, in a splendor unbelievable to most of us outside an Arabian night's dream. On another evening about a dozen of us dined at the palace with the Maharajah's brother, the Juvarajah, since the Maharajah's religious practices did not permit him to eat with non-Hindus. A vast, magnificent room with a table elaborately set, gold plate, a liveried servant behind each chair, a succession of courses and wines—the whole thing had my head spinning with the contrasts I was experiencing.

A couple of weeks later I found myself near Madura at the All-India student conference spending a week sitting on stone floors. Meals were served on the floor of long, stone-paved corridors, covered, but open to rain and sun on the side. A large banana palm leaf was placed before each person. A barefoot Indian servant moved along the line carrying a huge metal pot of rice, from which he placed a portion on each leaf. After him came five or six servants carrying smaller pots, each containing a different curry. We watched our hosts delicately mix a bit of curry and rice with the finger-tips and convey it skillfully to their mouths. I had read that polite usage required that one not dip in deeper than the second joint of the finger, but I always had the impression that I was getting involved almost to my elbow. Most difficult of all for me was that the food was so "hot." Some of the curries were so highly seasoned that my whole insides felt scalded and I learned to leave those untouched on my leaf. I never ceased to wonder how the internal organs of the Indian students were able to deal apparently successfully with these "blistering" seasonings, meal after meal and day after day. A banana was usually served with the meal and I alternated bites of banana and curry to dampen the flames somewhat.

This whole tale reminds me of a European I knew who once said, "I believe that I am making some progress at developing an international mind, and am perhaps beginning to develop an international heart, but as for an international stomach . . . I give up."

It was decades later when it began to dawn on me that all of these striking contrasts in passions for food were my first lessons in relative reality. The "value" lay not in the substance but in the mind of the one experiencing the substance. Even today my nose closes and my stomach turns as I recall an experience with a tropical fruit called a durian. In Singapore I learned that some animals were so passionately attached to the durian that they would lie in wait beneath a tree for hours or even days in order to devour one when it fell. And if several animals were frantically grasping for the same one, they even killed one another in the fight for this prize.

To my amazement, I learned that some humans shared this passion for the durian, and considered it a priceless delicacy. I found this difficult to believe, having read the following definition of a durian: A tropical fruit with the consistency of a thick custard, smelling heavily of onions, and as if it had been pressed through a gas pipe in a mortuary!

No doubt this definition filled my mind as I was given my first taste of a durian. The definition struck me as exact in every detail—onions, gas, and formaldehyde. I felt sure I would vomit if I swallowed it and so I promptly spit out the precious substance. Today that experience helps me to comprehend the view of modern physics which sees the observer as part of the transaction between the observer and the observed.

I must tell you how we traveled in India. We three American women made long train trips covering thousands of miles of this vast sub-continent. Along with a succession of Indian women, we rode in "compartments" which were bare rooms, along the walls of which were hung rows of beds like folding shelves which we pushed up against the wall in the daytime. Believe it or not, we three had acquired twenty-two pieces of luggage, and when we reached a destination we hung out the window of the compartment seeking "char" (four) bearers. Many of the pieces they carried on their heads.

From home we had each taken a bed roll consisting of

blankets, sheets, and pillow (this was before the days of sleeping bags and no bedding was supplied on the trains). We each had also a large duffle bag containing several months' supply of every conceivable necessity, including Kotex squashed as much as possible. Our suitcases held clothing and shoes for all extremes of climate and for all occasions including dressing for dinner on ships and elsewhere (I carried four evening dresses!). Unfortunately for us, wash-and-wear garments were not yet even a gleam in the eye of their inventors, so we carried traveling irons and extra supplies of clothes because laundry facilities were uncertain and often non-existent. Amost anything you can imagine, we were carrying.

In Bombay we added a portable covered wash basin and a "tiffin" basket for food en route. I can still feel the pang of homesickness which took hold of me in a strange Indian market filled with the sights and smells of unknown foodstuffs, when I found cans (tins!) of California peaches and Monterey sardines. (Now, fifty years later, India has greatly changed and the sardines have left Monterey bay.)

By the time we left India I, normally buoyant in temperament, was almost in a depression. Nothing could have prepared me for the suffering I saw everywhere, nor for the hopelessness I felt as I witnessed its magnitude. Bearing heavily on me, too, was the profound lassitude and hopelessness I sensed among the people. I did not see where the energy could come from to make the changes which appeared to me so essential. I saw no way for the outer needs to be met and, at that time, I did not meet people whose inner resources were such that I could see great hope in their answers. Nor did I myself then have any concept of an inner resource or an overview which could profoundly affect my understanding of all that I was seeing. I left India, a chastened Westerner whose customary "ideas of progress" had been found wholly inapplicable to another culture.

One day on a ship between Singapore and Hong Kong, Erma had reason once again to say in her kindly way that no Californian should have been chosen for such a journey since we obviously had no experience with extremes of temperature. I always felt the heat and cold more than those who were accustomed to them. On this day, the Indian bath steward had come to tell me that my bath was drawn, which meant that I would slosh around in a deep tub of warm salt water using a special soap, while hoping that the sea was not so rough as to make the water spill over the top. On arriving back at the tiny stateroom, I said to Juliette and Erma, "Don't come near me. I think I may have broken out in some contagious oriental disease. But just take a look at my rear." Whereupon Erma burst into loud laughter, proclaiming, "It's nothing but prickly heat!"

On landing in Hong Kong, the contrast between the Indians and the Chinese struck me forcibly. Instead of the low level of energy, the lassitude and resignation I had become accustomed to in India, the Chinese coolies came swarming energetically on board to collect the luggage, shouting animatedly, gesturing and shoving in a frenzy of activity. I marveled at the difference, and wondered.

And yet I am immediately reminded to jump ahead to another bit of relativity, for when I left China after about seven weeks, having traveled inland the length of the country to Mukden in Manchuria, I had another striking contrast presented to me. Japan was at that period on the march and had taken over Korea. The train on which I was to travel south, traversing the length of Korea, was therefore a Japanese train. I made my way into the diner for lunch, and now here I am looking out at a barren, cold landscape, where people's picturesque dress is different from anything I have ever seen. Suddenly a Japanese waiter comes running down the aisle towards the table where I am seated, and rushes past me. I turn around, asking myself, "Where's the fire?'' At that moment another waiter hurries from behind me and rushes in the opposite direction. This goes on until I feel like someone at a tennis match, my head turning first one way and then the other, as the Japanese waiters rush past me and I try to figure out what is going on. Finally I am forced to a very uncomfortable conclusion: There isn't any fire; there isn't any unseen crisis. These waiters are simply going about the business of serving a meal with Japanese efficiency. The only problem is that I have come from weeks in the interior of China and I am encountering an outpost of modern industrialized, militarized Japan. I have imperceptibly taken on the pace, the rhythm of the China of 1929 and I am now caught up in a new, different, rather frightening pace.

So let me go back to those remarkable weeks in China. Except for England, to which I felt drawn by roots of familiarity and family, I was more deeply drawn to China than to any area I touched on the journey. I loved China and after returning home I recall feeling that if I could go back to China with someone I knew and loved, I could happily feel at home to live there.

Juliette and Erma and I spent some time in Canton and Shanghai, and then we parted, they to return to the United States and I to travel alone in China and Japan. Because of our connections with the student YWCA, we were welcomed by staff members of the world YWCA in various countries, and these contacts enormously enriched our experiences. They also facilitated practical logistics of travel which would have been impossible otherwise.

So the day came when I (now with one suitcase and an overnight bag) went aboard a small boat for a four-day journey up the Yangtze to Hankow-Wuchang (this probably takes an hour or two in a plane in modern China). I was en route to Changsha in Hunan province, which later became famous because Mao Tse-tung had his youth and schooling there.

The reason for all of this went back to Berkeley and the student YWCA which helped to support the work of Maud Russell, a young American woman who had recently graduated from the University of California, had learned Chinese and was now in Changsha. There she gathered together a group of Chinese women who started some basic activities as a YWCA. Maud was a "character" then, and still is, in her mid-eighties in New York, where she edits the *Far East Reporter* and gives enthusiastic support to The People's Republic of China, whose guest she has been several times in recent years.

I had never met Maud, but she learned that I would be in China en route home from the India meetings, and invited me to visit her. To make things easier for me, she met me in Hankow and we traveled together down to Changsha by overnight train.

Those next two weeks were priceless. Maud lived alone, very simply, in small quarters on two floors, almost in Chinese style. She wore Chinese dress, the long padded cotton garments so practical in the cold weather and the essentially unheated houses. Each evening someone brought containers of hot water from which we took baths in a small portable metal tub. Our breakfasts and suppers were simple Chinese meals. At mid-day we walked over to the compound of "Yale-in-China," which included a medical center and a small staff of Americans who practiced and who trained Chinese medical personnel. We shared an American style meal with this group each day.

One day I happened to be walking alone to the compound for lunch. The street I was on was only a few feet wide and all at once a rickshaw came hurtling toward me. In it rode a man in an informal sort of soldier's "uniform," whose head was bleeding through a crude bandage. Behind him ran men whose clothing was distinguished by bits of cloth pinned on with safety pins and which seemed to serve as a kind of insignia. I pressed against the wall to allow them to pass, and went on to the Yale compound.

There I learned to my stupefaction that the city had been taken over by revolutionary troops and that I had encountered a remnant of the fleeing "army" which was leaving the city to the forces coming up from the south. All rail communication was cut off, and no one had any idea what might happen next.

Actually it turned out that there was a minimum of dislocation for the population this time, although there was no outside communication.

For me personally, a strangely idyllic period of time followed which seemed outside of time and space as I knew it. We didn't know when I would be able to leave Changsha, if ever, but the season was Chinese New Year and we settled into a calm, nourishing time of making New Year calls on many Chinese families, of walking through the city, of talking and reading and appreciating what *was*.

It was in this time that I began to see how a person may come to learn another language. A flood of Chinese language poured over me as we made our New Year visits, and a time came when I began to sense at least what subject they were discussing. We passed hours in one home or another.

Beautifully presented special sweets were offered, but I particularly enjoyed watching the dainty skill of the Chinese ladies as they ate watermelon seeds. It was an art I never mastered. What it required was to manipulate the tongue and front teeth in a way to make a length-wise crack in the seed (not to smash it to bits as I tended to do) after which a deft rolling of the tongue separated hull from kernel. The kernel was then chewed appreciatively, the hull having been dextrously spat upon the stone floor. It was a marvelous accomplishment which I could admire but could not emulate.

One evening Maud and I walked along a narrow dirt road between a number of very poor, dirty hovels and muddy yards. When we emerged and I could breathe again I exclaimed, "How can they stand living in that smell?"

Maud's reply was, "What smell?" Thus my lessons in relativity continued.

Well, I cannot stay on in Changsha indefinitely, then or now. After a couple of weeks, the trains ran again, and the city accustomed itself to the ground-swell of revolution which continued to gather strength as the years passed. Because I saw and heard and felt and smelled the conditions of the people in the old China, I have felt a lively interest in the development of the People's Republic of China. When I was at last able to visit it recently, I could and did appreciate the astonishing changes which have been brought about, at whatever cost, in the new.

In February 1929, Maud Russell finally put me aboard a northbound train and after several days of travel I reached Peking, where I was able to spend two memorable weeks. Now when I think of Peking I remember above all the beautiful circular Temple of Heaven, with its deep blue tiles and its carved marble terraces. It seemed to me then a perfect symbol of human aspiration reaching for the heights, an aspiration which a part of me shared profoundly.

Then a stay in Manchuria, at Mukden, and the transition to the tempo of the Japanese train I told you about.

Japan itself was full of beauty and my contacts with its people were uniformly kind and helpful. I recall a narrow-minded cliché which was going the rounds in those days. It said categorically, "All Chinese are dirty and honest and all Japanese are clean and dishonest." I cannot even imagine where such generalizations originate and I am ashamed to be remembering and repeating this one. I do recall being aware of how much my perceptions were determined by the fact that my travel was in the direction of India to Burma to Malaysia to China to Japan, and not in the inverse order. As it was, Japan seemed "clean and westernized," although I deeply appreciated the ancient, oriental aspects.

One of the most magnificent examples of natural and

man-made beauty is Nikko, to which I was to journey alone from Tokyo. My American hostesses took me to the train station where we could see the train waiting on the other side of the barrier. I assured them that there was no need to buy platform tickets and see me into my seat, since with the train staring me in the face, I could not possibly go wrong.

But once again, ha ha ha!!! I walked along the train, selected a likely-looking coach and got aboard. A couple of hours out of Tokyo, the conductor came along to collect the tickets. Consternation, uncertainty, much Japanese and no communication except that we both kept saying "Nikko" but with different intonations. After a time the conductor went away and returned with a young boy wearing the navy blue and white polka-dot kimona of a student. He said in English, "If-you-speak-ve-ry-slow-ly, I-think-I-can-un-der-stand." Thus proceeded a painful conversation in which I learned that only two cars of that train in the Toyko station had been destined for Nikko, and it was one of those I should have entered. They had earlier been dropped off and switched to a side-track for Nikko, while I was lurching rapidly into northern Japan, as night was closing down. I knew little Japanese except "Thank you" and "Goodbye" and I had the feeling I was going to need them both. I had no idea what would happen next.

What then transpired was typical of the courteous, kind, concerned treatment I received again and again in Japan. The plan was that at the next stop, I would get off, wait for the next train back to the junction, and there take the next train which was headed for Nikko. To make all of this as comfortable and painless as possible, the conductor carried my little overnight bag off the train and escorted me into the station-master's office where a warm stove was burning. This man thoughtfully telephoned to the hotel in Nikko to say that I was arriving on the last train, and he put me aboard the southbound train and asked the conductor to put me off at the junction. This he did, and saw me into a warm place to wait, from which I was once again put safely on the Nikko-bound train. Since Nikko was the end of the line, they knew that I couldn't get lost any further. This kind of thoughtful treatment was almost overwhelming as I experienced it and as I pictured the complications which could have occurred without it. Even now I am moved to recall that warmth and kindness to a lost young foreigner.

In April, on a twelve-day voyage from Tokyo to Seattle on a rough Pacific Ocean, I had the chance to sort out some of what had happened to me since I had left home the previous September. There had been so much to learn about division and unity, about differences and oneness, about what people think is important and unimportant, sacred and profane.

It had been a disappointment to me to find that my final voyage home to the United States would be via the northern route to Seattle. I had pictured a stop in glamorous Hawaii, with the journey ending as my ship sailed romantically through the Golden Gate (no bridge then!) into San Francisco bay. But the decision had been made that I should make stops in the Pacific Northwest, to give talks to students at the University of Washington and Washington State College, and then at the University of Oregon and Oregon State College before visiting colleges in California and Arizona.

So, one part of my time on shipboard was spent in thinking about those talks and about what I might have to say to young men and women interested in their part in this planet we share with so many different kinds of people. I had again and again been impressed by the forces which separate people and make them strangers and even enemies. I had thought deeply about what must be the nature of any force strong enough to unite them.

One such poignant moment had come early in the voyage to India. Students from Europe and America who were en route to the meeting of the World Student Christian Federation were getting acquainted and beginning to try to bridge some of the gaps of history, culture, and language. It was November 11, 1928, ten years from the day of the signing of the armistice which had ended the bloody years of World War I. Here we were, Germans, Austrians, French, British, Canadians, Americans and others, ready to observe the three minutes of silence at eleven in the morning. The ship stopped in the middle of the sunlit open Mediterranean Sea; the ship's bell chimed eleven, and our shared silence began. . . . The impact of that moment of unity still moves me deeply.

Other moments came during the India meeting. I had been amazed to learn the gulfs which appeared to separate the student groups which were in their countries the branches of the World Student Christian Federation. In the student YMCA's and YWCA's of the United States, while there was wide disparity of views in different geographical areas, the prevailing coloration was a somewhat superficial "social gospel" approach to religion. I was therefore astounded to encounter, for example, the Calvinistic doctrines of Karl Barth. As someone tried to interpret this to me, it was, "You were born in sin, you are living in sin, and you are about to die in sin, and there isn't a thing you can do about it!" That some of my contemporaries could believe this, was almost too much for my mind to encompass.

When we were at last in the sessions, and all of the nations who were to be represented had arrived, our differences of religion, politics, race, and cultures often seemed stronger than our similarities. For this reason I was deeply touched by an experience we shared a number of times. These moments came when each one, in his or her own language and version, repeated in unison the Lord's Prayer. This was probably one of my first realizations of the power of oneness.

Before finishing this segment about the trip around the world, I'd like to tell you a little about one of its greatest gifts to me. This was the opportunity to travel for several months, from London to Shanghai, with Juliette Derricotte. She was a beautiful black woman who at the time was on the staff of the National Student Council of the YWCA, living in New York and traveling in the colleges throughout the country. I came to think of her as a person who was pure gold, as if all of the dross had been burned out of her by her experiences as a Negro woman in the United States. She had seen and felt so much that the bitterness was burned away and she could view her life from a perspective unavailable to a person still totally caught in his or her own personal sufferings.

Her impact on the Indian students was tremendous. Juliette and a black YMCA staff member, Frank Wilson, were among our group of six Americans. The Indian students told them that they were the first Westerners they had ever met who could really understand their situation in relation to the British. Juliette taught them Negro spirituals, and later when we visited colleges in northern India and in Rangoon, we heard these students singing American Negro spirituals which they had taught to their classmates.

I recall a moment in one of our Indian train compartments. A big racial problem at the time was that of the Anglo-Indians, persons of mixed racial background who were not accepted by the Europeans and who refused to identify themselves as Indians. An Anglo-Indian woman traveling in our compartment obviously thought Juliette was an Indian, and snubbed her coldly and systematically. Some time later when she learned that Juliette was an

American Negro, her attitude shifted completely and she treated her as a fascinating anomaly, a kind of cultural artifact.

Jule told Erma and me later that it reminded her of an episode she had witnessed in a railroad station in the deep South in the United States. She saw an East Indian man being forcibly ousted from the "White" waiting room and steered toward the "Colored" waiting room. When he asserted his identity as a citizen of India, the officials apologized profusely and guided him back to the "White" area.

Once when Juliette spoke of her own travel in the South, she said that even up to that time she was physically afraid any time she was in Mississippi or in Texas. One day when we were on board ship, not long before we were to reach Hong Kong, she and I were leaning against the rail, talking. We had been traveling second class on some ships which left much to be desired, and I began to fantasize to Jule about the joys of getting on the American ship S.S. President Lincoln which we would take en route to Shanghai, after some time in Canton. I was dreaming of American coffee, and waffles, and of fresh fruit at the beginning of breakfast instead of tinned or stewed fruit at the end. And I dreamed of a one-class ship with decent deck space to walk in.

Something in Juliette's response brought to me a flood of realization that getting back into an American setting was a completely different experience for her than for me. I said something which indicated my painful awareness of what she was facing, and she replied, "Oh, don't feel too badly, Fran. There are worse things than being black." Then she looked far off to the horizon and said quietly, almost as if to herself, "What are they?"

Juliette had been born in Athens, Georgia, had graduated from Talladega College and then earned a Master's degree at Columbia. She had enjoyed living in New York, with

relative freedom from the then Jim Crow laws of the South.
However, before we left for India, she had made the decision to move back to the South. She had accepted the position of Dean of Women at Fisk University in Nashville,
Tennessee.

I was so deeply moved by all of the experiences of our
journey and by my view of the American racial situation
through Jule's eyes, that I was seriously considering a future
with an emphasis on doing something about race relations.
We even talked about whether I could be admitted to Fisk
to do some graduate work. I didn't know whether a white
person would be allowed. This has just brought to mind
something which Juliette said to me, and which seemed at
the time the finest compliment I had ever received. She
said, "There isn't any group in the country that I wouldn't
be willing to take you into."

From Shanghai we went our separate ways. You will be
hearing in the next chapter about the strange turn in my
life; Juliette went to Fisk University as planned. In her
second year there, she and some friends were driving for
the weekend to her family's home in Georgia. There was a
head-on crash with another car. Juliette and another black
woman were seriously injured and during the night were
driven from one hospital to another but were refused ad-
mittance. They both died.

Coming home on the ship to Seattle I was not the same
girl who had left Berkeley, nor would I ever be again. As it
happened, I was ready for a big leap in consciousness, and
it came, prepared for in part by those months as a foreigner
in so many strange, different places.

One of those experiences has just flashed into my mind,
and it is one which made a deep impression on my view of
the mind-body relationship. This phenomenon was presented to my consciousness at a religious festival of Tamil
Indians, originally from South India but then living in

Singapore. On this day in Singapore I watched a parade of men who were in a kind of religious ecstacy and fervor. Their bodies were bare to the waist, and were covered with an ashy powder. Some of them had, down their backs, two long rows of huge safety pins several inches long pinned through the skin, to each of which was attached a metal weight. Others had high above their heads large metal objects which were held up by a number of long, pointed spears pierced into the body, front and back. Not a drop of blood was visible anywhere.

These men moved on to a place where a bed of red hot coals, about twenty feet in length, had been prepared. They calmly walked the length of these burning coals with no indication of pain, and reached the other side with no sign of a burn on the soles of their feet.

No wonder I was ready to look at some new possibilities for the expansion of consciousness. And no wonder that, many years later when "paranormal abilities," holistic health, and the interrelationship of body, mind, and spirit began to seem credible, I had in my own experience some striking hints of the possibilities which already exist in our consciousness.

CHAPTER 7

The Asilomar Bridge to
Camp Minnesing

I WAS AT MY parents' home in Berkeley on my twenty-second birthday, April 24, 1929. It seemed a particularly joyful occasion and I was warmed by the love of friends and family. Then came an extended visit to some of the colleges in southern California and Arizona. Finally in mid-June, as a kind of completion of my responsibility to report to the student associations which had sent me to the India meetings, I went to the annual conference for the southwestern region of the National Student Council of the YWCA. This was always held at Asilomar, a conference center in an extraordinarily beautiful bit of the coast on the Monterey Peninsula. It combines white sand dunes, pines and gnarled cypresses, and the Pacific Ocean in all its moods. To me it had been a place of inspiration since my first conference there as a Girl Reserve in 1923. Once again, Asilomar was to be the setting for a further step in the evolution of my consciousness.

The theme of the ten-day conference that year centered around an effort to go behind some of the Christian "ideas about" Jesus in order to try to understand more directly the person himself, around whom so many diverse beliefs had grown up over the centuries. One of the leaders who had been invited to help in this search was Dr. Henry Burton Sharman, the "question asker" I mentioned in Chapter 2.

Dr. Sharman was a man whose personality seemed somewhat reserved and forbidding. He had grown up in the latter part of the nineteenth century, a Canadian whose brilliant, incisive mind had, as he studied to be a chemist, rejected any possibility of truth in religion. Later he saw the possibility of discovering, beneath the later Christian overlay, some historical facts about the man Jesus, which might differ from the traditional picture and might be of great significance for the present. He had plunged with characteristic thoroughness into a study of the field, including the ancient languages of the source materials, and had completed, in 1909, a nine-year doctorate at the University of Chicago. My view is that if his dissertation, "The Teaching of Jesus about the Future," were studied with a fully open mind, it would revolutionize a lot of things —but that is not my primary interest nor was it Dr. Sharman's.

His interest was to make it possible for an open mind to explore the life and teaching of a man who has profoundly affected Western thought. Dr. Sharman had acquired a remote, beautiful camp in northeastern Canada, in Algonquin Park north of Toronto, and had begun leading summer seminars for groups of about thirty men and women who were willing to examine, critically and historically, the records we have about the young Jew, Jesus.

Before going on to this Camp Minnesing in the summer of 1929, Dr. and Mrs. Sharman attended the student conference at Asilomar. He led a ten-day group of which I was a member, using the same general method which he used in his Canadian summer seminars. The required attitude of mind was one of openness and scientific inquiry, setting aside as far as possible one's previously held beliefs and preconceptions from whatever source. The text was Dr. Sharman's *Records of the Life of Jesus,* an ingenious but simple three-column presentation which Dr. Sharman had made to allow one to examine and compare the three related accounts which are known as Matthew, Mark, and Luke. Dr. Sharman did no lecturing. He asked questions. He asked them endlessly and penetratingly, and he expected group members to find the answers by examining, with new eyes and open minds, the evidence before them in the text.

It was the most exhilarating and stimulating intellectual exercise I had ever been involved in. I was fascinated to recognize the beliefs I had held uncritically, having absorbed them from my environment, even though mine had been a minimally "Christian" one. And I could see and hear the others struggling with the assumptions they held. I marveled as they, too, looked at the accounts critically as literary, historical documents, and found something quite different from their hitherto unquestioned preconceptions.

Beyond this was the further step of looking at what appeared to be the central teaching of this exceptional young man, repeated again and again in different forms. I began to see the parallel between the state of openness and willingness required by Dr. Sharman's method of study, and that required for the conduct of one's life—that is, the voluntary letting go of specific expectations of how things "should" be according to a restricted personal viewpoint, and the moving into a willingness to embrace What Is, seen from an expanded, inclusive viewpoint.

The whole thing was intriguing and astounding to me. Our group met all morning each day of the Asilomar conference and I could scarcely wait for the next "installment."

It was like watching a serial. After about a week, Dr. Sharman quietly mentioned to me one day after lunch that if I would like to do it, he and Mrs. Sharman would be very pleased to have me come to the summer seminar at Camp Minnesing as their guest.

Wow! What an opportunity! For an instant it glowed like giant fireworks in a night sky, and then I replied, "What a wonderful possibility! Of course you know how I have loved the work in the group and how I would welcome the chance to go more deeply. I appreciate the generous offer, but I really can't possibly go away from home so soon again, after having been away from my family for so long." Dr. Sharman accepted my answer and said that he understood.

The day after the conference was over, a few of the leaders had stayed on, and I was with them. One of these was a lovely man, Allan Hunter, minister of a liberal church in Hollywood which attracted many young people. Allan had a deep interest in social action and non-violent means of working toward it. His wife, Elizabeth Hunter, had with me been one of the members of Dr. Sharman's study group during the preceding ten days. We three sat talking by the fire in their bedroom in the rustic old Lodge at Asilomar, when Elizabeth announced to me, "Frances, I have a divine inspiration! I think you should go to Camp Minnesing this summer."

I laughed. "That's not such a divine idea. The Sharmans already had that one and I decided against it."

"No," continued Elizabeth, "I really mean it. I saw how you were attracted to his method, and I think that right now is the time to go on with it. You've had a glimpse of something, but a whole summer at Minnesing could make all the difference to you."

Deep down, I knew she was right. The Sharmans were by then on a transcontinental train somewhere in the middle west. I sent a telegram to them on the train, asking if the invitation was still open. They wired a warmly welcoming reply. In July, therefore, I once more boarded a train and headed for what turned out to be the most determinative experience of my life.

Well, we have now reached the place where you are free to say, "This is where we came in." And it is true; we have made the circle back to that summer of 1929 at Camp Minnesing, where I learned about willingness and had the two canoe experiences I described for you in Chapter 2. The setting for all of this was a cluster of cedar log cottages on the shores of a quiet lake in the Canadian woods. There was a rough, barely defined wagon road on which supplies reached it from a little railroad line, but all of the people came in from another direction, six miles by canoe, with three overland portages. By the time we arrived we had already begun to move into another world.

Seven days a week, from nine to one with a mid-morning break, we sat in a circle in the seminar room and answered Dr. Sharman's questions. As we grew more accustomed to what appeared to be some of the literary relationships between the accounts which are entitled Matthew, Mark, and Luke, we began to have a basis for some discrimination as to the probable authenticity or lack of authenticity in certain passages or phrases. Also, under Dr. Sharman's rigorous and sometimes ruthless questioning, I began to see the outlines of, to me, a new and strikingly different picture of this young man as he functioned in his milieu, apparently from an unusual kind of inner authority.

As I explained in the second chapter on "How I Learned About Willingness," the heart of the study was our effort to comprehend the meaning of a number of different sayings attributed to Jesus when he was asked, "What must I do to fulfill my life?"

I've told you how I understood that answer, when I was twenty-two. In essence, what it called for from me was to put one thing first in my life. It was a choice to substitute one single allegiance in the place of all others. It was to want one thing. At that time I thought of it as something general, something outside of myself which I identified as the "will of God" and which I left undefined until I met it in a specific situation. As far as I was able, my commitment to it was total and was given in advance of and apart from particular actions. My allegiance was wholehearted and put me in a state of willingness to move in WHATEVER direction might be called for.

You know what happened in the two canoe experiences. It is important for me to communicate to you the fact that what led me to take this drastic step ("lose my life") was an avid hunger for the most expanded life I could find. This motivation, which is a universal, evolutionary drive, was sufficient to make me take the plunge into the unknown. I thought that this transformational process sounded unlikely and scary, but I was impressed by the results that were offered. I decided to meet the condition. In the canoe experiences I chose to want one thing, and I learned the meaning of willingness in the midst of acute inner conflict. I was astonished at the new level of life I found. I thought I had arrived. I discovered that I had just begun.

CHAPTER 8

The Middle Years, Part I
After the Big Change . . . What?

L OOKING BACK OVER the fifty years between 1929 and
1979, I am impressed by the significance of my relationships with three individuals, a woman and two men,
who were markedly different from one another yet had this
in common: each one possessed qualities that were almost
the mirror-opposite of those that I recognized and
accepted in myself. All were introverts; all were uncomfortable at expressing themselves in groups of people; all
tended to see people and events from a somewhat pessimistic, negative point of view, believing that a "realistic"
view was one which essentially expected the worst rather
than the best. On each of these three I unawarely projected
an unowned, unaccepted side of myself.

The first was a young woman I met in Berkeley when I
returned from Dr. Sharman's seminar in the fall of 1929.
The second was a man I later met through Dr. Sharman,

whom I loved and expected to marry. The third was my husband, Bert Horn, whom I married in 1937.

Anne was in two of my classes when I re-enrolled at the University of California to complete the final semester of undergraduate work I had missed when I was laid low by strep throat. I was still walking on air after the two canoe experiences at Camp Minnesing and was trying to realize that I now formed the third side of a radically different kind of "triangle" with the man I had been with in the canoe, and his wife. I knew that my love for him was without demands or possessiveness and presented no threat whatever to his wife. It was unconditional love and I thought it was wonderful.

As I began to know Anne, the young woman in Berkeley, I sometimes tried to tell her in a general way about this new way of life I had learned, but nothing much happened. One day when she was feeling depressed because members of her family were caught in bitter jealousies and apparently destructive marital triangles, I told her that I knew three people who had a remarkable relationship, free of jealousy and possessiveness.

I said, "I know that it really happened for these people, and no one is threatened or frustrated." Anne scoffed at the idea, saying that such a state of affairs between a man and two women was quite impossible. I said no more.

Some weeks later when I knew her better, I told this new friend that I was the girl in that triangle. Amazingly, in a flash, that personal revelation illuminated the ideas I had been trying to convey to her about letting go, allowing, surrendering to some higher "will" which could direct one's life. Suddenly, as exemplified in a living, breathing person who had experienced this unusual human relationship, she saw the transformational process with perfect clarity and precipitated herself into it.

For me this was like another miracle when I watched the remarkable changes which began to take place in Anne as she increasingly found a supportive, steadying centeredness in the willingness state. It was also a great gift to me to have someone who understood and appreciated the new state I had found, and we explored it together. Anne, of course, wanted to go to Camp Minnesing the next summer, and we did that for four succeeding summers.

Meanwhile, in January 1930, when I had finished my B.A. in psychology, I embarked on a year-and-a-half of work on an M.A. thesis entitled, "A Psychological Study of the Dominance of a Generalized Desire over Specific Desires" (Horn, 1931). During a year of this time Anne was in Europe with another friend and I immersed myself in the transformational process as I found it in the seventeen individuals I was studying in depth for my thesis.

At the time, nothing seemed to me more important than to state clearly what was involved in this shift in inner direction. Now, fifty years later, the importance of this transformation strikes me more forcibly than ever, both for its integrative, expansive effect for the individual and for its determinative effect for the human species. This time I can offer to you seventy-four years of my own life to illustrate what happens when I want one thing and what happens when I fail to do that. The difference in results is the difference between heaven and hell.

In May 1931, having received the M.A. in psychology, one obvious possibility for my future would have been to take a job as secretary of a student YWCA at some university. I did have offers of that kind. However, by this time what seemed all-important was to find ways to communicate the central idea that I had discovered through Dr. Sharman's method of the critical, historical study of his arrangement of the *Records of the Life of Jesus*. A number of faculty members who taught in a variety of fields in some Canadian and American universities were already leading such groups in their homes, as an avocation.

What now transpired came about for the very practical reason that both of Anne's parents had died shortly before I met her, and she had a substantial independent income. With "God's gold," as she euphemistically called it, we could both go to some university campus to lead the "Records" groups with students and faculty, without my having to be tied to a job.

We decided on Stanford University and went there in the fall of 1931, where we spent two years leading faculty and student groups in the Records, and later did something similar for two more years at UCLA. Each summer we spent six weeks at Camp Minnesing at Dr. Sharman's seminar, and in the winters we pursued some additional, more detailed individual study with Dr. Sharman in California, where he and Mrs. Sharman had moved. Our interests were deeply involved with the people we met through all of these contacts.

One of these was Robert, whom I came to know through Dr. Sharman. We "fell in love" and were expecting to marry. Anne and I both saw something of him, although he lived a continent away. We all shared this basic interest in finding our way on our individual, challenging transformational journeys. Anne and Robert and I were painfully learning that our years of conditioned behavior did not vanish like the mist before the morning sun after the initial change in our life-direction. Our rigid responses tended to continue despite our glimpses of the freedom and zest we experienced when we were in a place of willingness, wanting the one thing.

For me, the pattern that dogged my footsteps on the new path was the deep self-rejection behind the superficial appearance of capability. I lived with the unrecognized belief that I had been found inadequate, unsatisfactory, "less than." To compensate, I needed to be not only "more than" but *the* best, *the* first. Instead of maintaining myself consistently at a relatively balanced level, something would seem to attack my vulnerable ego and I would plunge down to minus 100. Then, instead of moving back up to a centered level, I often shot on up to plus 100, or if possible to plus 1,000, to overcome the sense of lack and of being "less than."

These yo-yo tactics of the uncentered self continued to go on during the time that I was trying to learn what it meant to let go of the hold on all of the specifics, and the sense of separateness, in order to attune to WHATEVER my expanded consciousness could see as appropriate, moment by moment.

Following a confused period in my relationship with Robert and with Anne, I was thrown into one of the most devastating experiences of my life. One day when Robert was in California for a visit, he said that he realized that it was Anne he loved, not me. I was demolished, destroyed. With my life-long pattern of deeply masked self-doubt and non-self-acceptance, you can picture the situation. I, who had a consuming need to be first, was suddenly not first with the two people I cared most about. I was deeply wounded and felt a victim of treachery on both their parts. I became enraged, fighting helplessly against a feeling of being wiped off the earth. There seemed to be nothing left, and I considered how to withdraw from the world, one way or another. Nothing of the 1929 level of consciousness seemed available to me.

The way out was to retreat into serious illness. I became acutely ill and the pain and weakness of my physical state made it impossible for me to lead groups as before. Anne was forced to take on, alone and at short notice, the leadership of the first month-long seminar we had planned to do together.

Following surgery and a prolonged, debilitating illness, I slowly began to find my way back. The relationships with Robert and with Anne were painfully broken. During all of this time I was feeling cut off not only from Robert and

Anne but from the wider group with whom I had been associated in the Records study.

During my convalescence I spent some time on the desert in southern California, where I met Bert Horn, to whom I was married for thirty years until his death on Christmas Eve, 1967.

If there are teaching marriages, this one must rank high as an educational experience for both of us. Bert and I were opposites in almost everything, and this fact led to richness and joys in our years together, as well as to agonizing pain. Obviously something deep in each one of us had chosen and continued to choose the other. But there were many times when each one of us seemed to the other an intolerable partner.

My relationship with Bert further widened the breach with the group I had previously been close to. He was interested to hear about the Records study but his cynicism (he called it realism) kept him from believing that the people I knew were sincerely committed to WHATEVER a centered inner direction might require. For example, he doubted that Anne recognized the power she wielded because of her money. Also, after meeting Dr. Sharman, Bert characterized him as a "rigid old bastard"! In fact, in one of his periodic efforts to get my feet down on the ground, he inquired provocatively, "And how do we know that there ever was such a guy as Jesus?"

When you hear these things, and many more to come, you have to ask what could have kept us together—and apart from my former interests and friends—for thirty years. The answer has been coming to me more clearly as I have been trying to put all of this together for you. It is apparent that something in me knew very well that I needed a different series of influences to balance all that had so engrossed me since the first summer at Camp Minnesing. And did I get them? Yes, I did!!

CHAPTER 9

The Middle Years, Part II
Nudism and Open Marriage

W HEN I FIRST met Bert he was recovering from serious tuberculosis of both lungs. He was disease-free, but was considered by the insurance company to be "totally and presumably permanently disabled." After an affluent childhood and youth, a series of losses had resulted in his being reduced to a tiny income and a small reserve, which he had painfully built up as he fought and clawed his way back to some semblance of health.

Bert's mother had died when he was about six; his step-mother embodied for him every imaginable negative quality, and this was intensified at his father's death when Bert was about seventeen, leaving the step-mother and two half-sisters. Later, Bert's first wife left him for another man while he was in bed for a year in the TB sanitarium. After all of this, I was astounded that Bert was even considering remarriage, but I had no idea of how our marriage would be affected by what Bert would be expecting of a woman.

After we began to discuss the possibility of marriage, Bert made it clear that he had no use for the concept of an "engagement." This was because an engagement was a promise, and he had decided that it was impossible to promise to love. He and his first wife had done that, "till death us do part," and it hadn't worked. So there were to be no promises to love. I remember how sometimes in later years Bert would announce cheerfully in the morning, "I love you today." The implication was clear—that I had better earn whatever love I would get tomorrow!

I marvel at the kind of negative self-image I had which let me accept such a statement. Yet I think that simultaneously I sensed in it something refreshing and true about living in the newness of the present moment as opposed to something deadened by habit. However, it was no doubt a far cry from an unconditional love which simply radiates from a center and falls equally upon the "just and the unjust!"

It's amazing to me as I write, how the memories come back from so long ago. I have just recalled another facet in the "educational program" which Bert provided for me. At the time I met him he had a woman friend who lived in another area and whom he saw occasionally, of whom he was fond, and with whom he had a sexual relationship. There were practical reasons, chiefly financial, why their marriage seemed an impossibility, and they had about reached the conclusion that each would look elsewhere for a partner. Bert had a real horror of the idea of jealousy, and he was encouraging this woman to marry a man she knew who would be able to support her and her rather frail health. He was in no condition to take care of her.

Also, as we grew closer together, Bert said that the only real test for jealousy was in a relationship which included the sexual. He wanted a wife who would not be jealous. Therefore, he would not marry me unless we had lived together sexually, which would allow him to test my freedom from jealousy! This all seems pretty bizarre as I write it, since it appears we both accepted the idea that it was only I who required a test. Actually I was almost incredibly naive and virginal, and I bowed to Bert's wider experience.

So, in a clandestine fashion, using a false name, I got in touch with a public "Mother's Clinic" in a rather poor neighborhood in Los Angeles, and went to be fitted for a diaphragm. I felt conflict over the whole thing, which went against my general cultural conditioning that a nice girl didn't have sexual relations until after marriage.

The months passed, and the sexual relationship became a part of our total experience together. Bert and the woman he had known intimately knew that their particular relationship was ending. Bert therefore suggested to me one day that he and I drive to where she lived, and that I amuse myself for the afternoon while he and she had the time alone to say goodbye to their relationship as it had previously been. I acceded, and this is what we did. Probably I thought that it was part of my "jealousy test."

One day in the months before we decided to marry, Bert asked, "What would you think of going to a nudist park?"

Amazed, I replied, "Why would anyone want to go to a nudist park?"

Bert answered, "Health."

He had been reading about the small camps that were being established, mostly on the east and west coasts, often by Germans who took an interest in physical fitness. Something he read about sunshine and TB made him think that nudism would be beneficial and he wanted to try it. "If you won't go with me, I'll go by myself."

I thought the idea was crazy and I felt very uneasy about the whole thing, but I was "in love" with Bert and if he was all for this, I would go too. He corresponded with a couple of the camps, and we knew we would go at some convenient time. Meanwhile, we decided to be married.

My family and some of my friends took a dim view of the plan. (Frances had been expected to marry a college president, at least.) But I was no prize at that moment, emerging as I was from prolonged and debilitating illnesses, with now the necessity to support myself and to contribute to our expenses as a couple. What to do? The time was mid-depression, and who wanted someone with an M.A. in psychology and no regular employment history? The answer at that moment was: The State Relief Administration, where I was given the assurance of a job as a case worker. On April 3, 1937, Bert and I were married.

On the Labor Day weekend following our marriage, we drove to a nudist park in the hills high above Lake Elsinore. After a succession of forbidding "No Trespassing" signs and locked gates we had been given instructions for opening, we proceeded through a half-mile or so of rather barren hills covered with low brush. At a final gate, the instruction was to ring for permission to enter. The clanging cowbell shattered the silence and we waited. A clothed man opened the gate for us, and from then on we faced a strange new world.

Before an hour had passed, I was saying to Bert, "What I can't get over is that it is all so *wholesome!*" We had passed a tent where a fat, motherly woman was cooking outside on a gasoline stove, and whatever it was she was stirring smelled temptingly good. Then I began to see the children—from toddlers on up—running around under the oak trees or jumping into the swimming pool, their little brown bodies obviously enjoying the complete freedom and naturalness of the setting.

Little by little I began to feel comfortable. We had reserved a tiny cabin in which we undressed. There was a moment similar to the plunge into icy water when we walked nude into the open air to join other people, but from then on, the only thing that would have felt totally out of place was to be clothed. It was a world of wonderful freedom, with the body responding to the warmth of the sun, the movement of a breeze, the coolness of water. In those early days of the nudist movement, the parks were totally "straight." Not a drop of alcohol was allowed, not even beer. It was understood that there was to be no bodily contact in public, even by married couples. It was all so pure that if one inadvertently bumped against someone else's body, as in a volleyball game, one quickly moved away. No nude dancing was allowed, and for the evening dances we were fully clothed.

All of this has changed, of course. Most nudist parks gradually opened to alcohol, and some to drugs. The nude beaches appeared, and all of this reflected a much more flexible view of conduct than had been evident earlier, in the United States.

For Bert and me, the nudist weekends and summer holidays were something we enjoyed for several years. Bert greatly appreciated the healthfulness, freedom and naturalness, but in particular he liked the fact of the absence of superficial, materialistic distinctions. We were down to basic equipment! One's acquired possessions were not visible, and the whole emphasis was on simply being what we were. Only first names were used, and it was not acceptable to ask any personal questions, including those about one's occupation or home or mode of life. It had an essentially *honest* character, that simple life in the camp, sleeping under the stars, and cooking out of doors.

What strikes me now is what a marvelous lesson it was in my growing understanding of relative realities. To enter a nudist park we either accept the reality system of people who believe that under certain conditions nudism is appropriate and "proper," or we refuse that reality system and perceive everything in a way which is totally different from the way it looks to a nudist. I was always amused by the fact that, since the nudist park was legal in the county where it had been established, and since the No Trespassing

signs around the fenced property were clearly evident, anyone who got in to try to take a look was breaking the law.
We could and did call the sheriff when "voyeurs" of this
kind got in, and the sheriff's job was to protect us from the
clothed interlopers. I recall, too, a moment one day in
town when, in a supermarket, I saw a woman who looked
vaguely familiar but whom I could not place. When she
called me by name I recognized her as someone I had met
in the nudist park, and I exclaimed, "Oh, I didn't recognize you with your clothes on!"

During the first seven years of our marriage, Bert did
not have a job, and this in itself tipped the balance of the
relationship away from the usual pattern of those times.
Although "totally and presumably permanently disabled"
—a categorization which was profoundly constricting—
Bert started back to college part-time, shifting from
engineering to sociology, a field in which he subsequently
earned B.A. and M.A. degrees and had a successful twenty
year career.

But in those first years after our marriage, economic
factors seemed to dictate that my jobs and my offers of
other more responsible and demanding jobs should be
determinative of where we lived and who our friends were.
My energies were very much in the outer, where I was
competing and achieving. In social groups I was the extra-
vert and Bert the introvert. This was a big problem between
us always. Despite my deep underlying self-doubt, I was at
home in social situations, liked people, and was outgoing
in nature. Bert did not feel the same ease with groups, with
the result that our tendencies went in opposite directions
and caused acute discomfort between us.

When Bert and I were getting to know one another in the
months before we were married, we shared an interest in
the ideas of Fritz Kunkel, a German physician and psychologist, whose "We Psychology" had an appeal to us

both. We attended Kunkel's first California seminar in the autumn of 1936, where I took prodigious notes. Other participants (who had the good sense to rest back and enjoy watching Kunkel's genuine, spontaneous presentation in all its freshness and immediacy) then asked for copies of my notes. Bert volunteered to type them if I would dictate them to the machine. Thus began several months of deep and penetrating discussions on many aspects of Kunkel's We Psychology, which led to our saying that we really "got married on the Kunkel notes."

One of Kunkel's ideas about the relationship between men and women was illustrated by a series of twelve concentric circles. According to Kunkel's view, in the outer circle one would have a great many members of the opposite sex, whom one knew in only the most casual fashion, as nodding acquaintances. In each one of the circles there were less representatives of the other sex, but one knew them more and more intimately as one approached the center. In the central circle, according to Kunkel, there was one person who represented the whole of the opposite sex. As a corollary to this he believed that, in mature relationships, sexual intercourse was limited to the one person in the central circle.

Bert and I had been married for about a year and a half when he said that he did not see any basis for this last conclusion of Kunkel's and he would like to find out for himself whether or not there could be sexual intimacy outside of the one relationship in the center. Wow!—here we go again.

Bert was an honest person who thought a lot, and deeply. He had a searching, inquiring mind which, ipso facto, doubted the truth of any statement, simply because it had been made. (Years later this gave him an advantage in the stock market because he took the much-to-be desired "contrary opinion" position, which goes against what "everybody else" is saying.) In this present situation he wanted to find out for himself. He asked me how I would feel if he were to go off for the night with a woman I will call Tanya.

Wow again!! I felt as though I had been struck in the solar plexus. I felt sick at my stomach. Immediately I thought, "What is the matter with me that he has to try this with someone else? How can I say Yes? But how can I say No?"

Bert said, and I believed him, that if I said No, he would not do it. He said he wanted nothing to interfere with our relationship but he wanted to know about that second circle. (As I write this, I am laughing and feeling that he was indeed born too soon.)

In all the years that I knew Bert, I think that he never understood or embraced what I see as the transformational process. He worked diligently to be honest with himself and to solve his many problems, but he never reaped the fruits of a wholehearted choice to embrace wholeness. He was always struggling to cope, as a separate self, or a collection of separate selves, with all that was presented to him to deal with. And life presented him with much which he experienced as intensely painful, physically and emotionally.

In those same years, I spent an immense amount of time on a similar level of trying to cope with problems as they appeared, but at times I was clear about what the central core of me wanted. In this instance about Tanya and the second circle I put myself on the horns of an impossible dilemma. Everything in me cried out against this experiment, and wanted to say No. And yet I was also wanting Bert's love and I knew that if I said No to this plan of his, it would do something negative and possibly disastrous to our marriage. He had put the burden of the decision entirely on me, and I had uncritically accepted that burden. How could I bear it if he went with her? How could I bear it if he didn't, because I had said No? I knew that willingness was called for, but how could I be willing?

I was trying to base my life on wanting one thing. I had had powerful experiences to tell me that this placed me in a level of consciousness that felt free, expansive, joyful, secure, and peaceful. I knew that a willingness to express wholeness . . . WHATEVER would put me into that level of consciousness. But how could I be willing? How could I get beyond the agonized cry that was tearing my insides apart and saying, "You see? He doesn't want you. You aren't enough. You are a failure. Once again you are being rejected because you are unworthy. This is just another proof of what you really know about yourself."

We discussed it over and over again, with storms of my tears (but never of anger; one of our problems was that we almost never fought). I cannot reconstruct all that was going on in me during those dark days. I was conscious of the need for "willingness" but I was probably feeling a minimum of identification with anything like wholeness, or even an undefined Best. It is far more likely that I was trying to be willing to agree to what Bert wanted to do, so that I might have slightly more assurance (but not much more) that giving him this freedom would deepen our own relationship. So I finally said that if this was what he wanted to try, it was all right with me.

A few days later I came home one evening to find a note saying that he had gone for the night with Tanya. I was flattened, literally. I lay on the floor, shaking all over for about an hour and a half. I felt that I could not bear what was happening to me, and I felt particularly helpless because I had assented to this monstrosity. I was experiencing the darkest hour of my life up to that moment. The personality-self that I identified myself as being was wiped out, and devalued into nothing. Someone else was being given a place that I had believed was uniquely "mine." How could I bear the rejection?

Finally I dragged myself into bed, but slept little. Each time I became conscious I pictured what was going on with

Bert and Tanya, and felt destroyed, annihilated. When Bert returned the next day I managed to welcome him. He was elated to feel so much more love for me because of the freedom he had been given.

However, as time went on and Bert continued to experiment with sex in the second circle, I would experience drastic reversals in my feelings, would wail that I could not tolerate such a situation, and would not. Whereupon Bert would say, "Ok, if that is the way you feel, this will be the end of it." And once again I would go through all the steps, and end up being unable to be the one to say, "I will not go on with our relationship if this is to be part of it." So I would say, "I don't know why this is the way you want it, but if it is, OK."

All of this time, as Bert continued to see Tanya from time to time, he was assuring me that of course such a plan worked both ways and that I was perfectly free to do my own experimenting with the second circle. Some weeks later, when Bert was away for a month at a seminar, I stumbled into a relationship with a man who worked in the office with me. Then for several years Bert and I were really into an "open marriage" although the term had not yet been coined. Other people came and went for each of us, while our own relationship left much to be desired. It seems now that we must have been almost totally unconscious. Certainly we had no realization of how we projected onto one another aspects which were not developed or recognized in ourselves. We were not whole in ourselves, and we looked to others to complete us.

Today as I look back at our marriage, I realize that my tendency has been to view my life then as having been completely "off the path," almost as though I had never had the canoe experiences or the subsequent times of willingness. Comments of Dr. Paul Brenner have helped me to recognize the willingness I was struggling to achieve in the midst of all the pain and conflict.

I have recalled an incident when Bert and I were vacationing at the nudist park and Bert wanted to invite Tanya to come up for a couple of days. When he suggested this, my heart sank and I felt the churning in the solar plexus which by then was all too familiar. Although Tanya was not beautiful in the face, she had a voluptuous figure with which I compared my own unfavorably. I agreed to his inviting her and she came. We had moved a single bed near to our double bed under the oak trees. When it was time to go to bed, Bert announced that he would sleep in the single bed and that Tanya and I would occupy the double bed. Another of the painful "belly-blows"! What could this mean except that Bert did not consider me his wife, would not sleep in our bed, and was concerned not with my feelings but with not hurting Tanya? Lying on one edge of that bed looking at the stars, I agonized at what my conception of willingness had got me into. I was not willing. I was not wholehearted. I knew that somehow there must be a kind of openness that could be wholehearted, but it seemed impossible.

Several years later, during the last of the relationships in which I was involved with another man, I was feeling its unsatisfactoriness and the problems in the relationship with Bert, and I was making a valiant effort to re-establish myself at my center. In those days I was not meditating; I gave only some sort of token recognition to the "spiritual" in me; I had no support system in the form of close friends with whom I discussed the things that had deeply concerned me in the years immediately following the 1929 experiences.

In spite of that aridity, I knew that I had to end the relationship with the other man I was seeing occasionally. I wrote him a long letter in which I told him this, and tried to explain my reasons. I described what "wanting one thing" meant to me, and said that when I was *willing* to give up our relationship I knew clearly that it was a correct decision for me, and one I could choose wholeheartedly to make.

The man saw no sense to my decision but agreed to it. His own pattern of relationships continued with others, but mine did not.

This period of an open marriage for Bert and me ended when Bert was threatened with drastic legal action by the husband of a woman he had been interested in. For him the dream of this kind of open marriage collapsed as being more hazardous and unrewarding than it was worth.

For me the conclusion of this experimentation came as a kind of numb release from the pain of the previous years. Deep within me I believed that Kunkel's view of a mature relationship was true. I knew that my investment in assorted other relationships had precluded my full participation in a relationship with Bert, and I knew that my sporadic efforts to make my relationship with Bert honest and complete had precluded any satisfactory relationship with the other men. So, the end of the open marriage was a relief, but it did not, ipso facto, make a mature marriage. We were still two individuals, feeling incomplete, and looking for fulfillment where it cannot be found.

A day came when Bert announced that it appeared that we were incompatible and perhaps we should be divorced. Once again I was faced with the specter of failure, and could not bear it. It was not really that I did not see how I could live without Bert but that I could not face my world, including my family and friends, as someone whose marriage had failed. I pleaded that we take some time before making the decision.

For several years before and after this, Bert suffered acutely from attacks of severe abdominal pain. He went to various specialists but no physiological explanation for the pain was ever forthcoming. It is probably typical of our relationship that when Bert said to me one time, "You make me sick," I accepted this as a statement of fact and bought the whole package. And neither one of us had enough sense to know that that was crazy, and that we were responsible for our own responses.

We tried a summer separation, painful and essentially unproductive. Later a plan developed for me to move into Los Angeles for a two-year clinical internship in psychiatric social work. We knew that if we should choose to be together after this, the additional graduate training would permit me to work near to our home, in the Department of Mental Hygiene.

This was another painful period, with a lot of learning. Bert did some work with a psychiatrist, and when I returned home I went into analysis.

Bert's pain dominated much of our attention for the remaining years, including three years of retirement. This aggravated a basic problem we had always had concerning dependency-independency needs, and it was one that we never resolved. As I look back, it seems that the whole thirty years was one long, luminous lesson in "the way that doesn't work," but I begin to see its teachings.

Because of his pain, Bert became interested in Ernest Holmes' Religious Science, and did whatever he could to get help for his problem in this way. I went along with his interest and we were using what we could understand of this kind of thinking.

A few years before we retired, Bert had suggested that we re-join the nudist association and begin to go to a different park, nearer to our home. We had stayed out of this activity for a number of years, first because of the lack of free time and of gasoline during World War II, and later because we felt that nudism might be a threat to our work, even though it was legal. We were both involved with clients and with the public in our work and had decided not to risk the complications of being labeled as nudists at that time. Later this seemed less important.

As before, we enjoyed the naturalness and freedom. On

hot summer afternoons after work, we often had the olympic-sized swimming pool to ourselves, and could then sit by it and relax with a picnic supper.

After retirement, we began to go to nudist parks in San Diego County. At one pleasantly located small park we tried to rent quarters for the summer, but found there were none except for a couple who would help in the kitchen and maintain the swimming pool. This we did.

The following summer we went to another park where we knew and liked the owners. This time we were hoping to rent quarters we could occupy while we decided on a place to move to as a new, permanent location. Once again, nothing available to rent. However, they needed help in the snack bar, and there was a trailer waiting for a couple who would take on those duties. It looked too formidable; this was a big park with many members and big crowds on weekends. However, we said that we would help, with particular responsibility for breakfasts and lunches.

Thus began my career as a short-order cook in a nudist park. I met my match in "eggs over-easy" which most people ordered for breakfast and which posed a big problem, considering the nature of the frying pans available and the dexterity required. Add to this the pressure of many hungry customers at once; bacon, ham and hashed brown potatoes to negotiate in a limited space; plus hot cakes to make and to cook, and I was often overwhelmed. If ever I could have used some centeredness it was at those times, but I was a long way from a conscious connection with Source or Wholeness or God.

Soon after we were installed for our summer jobs, Bert was found to have cancer of the bladder. Then followed six months of nightmare in the hospital, with drastic surgery, radiation, and chemotherapy. It was a time of anguish for us both and it contained none of the wisdom that now is available for those facing cancer and facing death. After the surgery, the surgeon forbade me to tell Bert that he had cancer and this went on for four months and was one of the most painful parts of a pain-filled time. When finally Bert again asked whether he had cancer, I said yes. He never again spoke the word, nor did we ever speak of death until the day, on the morning of Christmas Eve, when he told me that he felt that he was dying. We expressed our love for one another and in effect said goodbye. I was alone with him a few hours later when he died.

CHAPTER 10

The Later Years

WHEN BERT DIED I was sixty years old. The period since that time has been for me what C.G. Jung called the "second half of life." All that had happened before, including Bert's death itself, somehow opened for me a whole new area of consciousness. The turn was inward.

At first there was a need to move slowly out of a state of almost total exhaustion, physically and emotionally. Bert and I had been in a town about one hundred and fifty miles away from our home at the time he was hospitalized. We had planned to move to that area, and had given preliminary thought to the sale of our small home. One day, when Bert's illness was far advanced, he suggested that it might seem easier if we were rid of the house. I could not imagine how I could possibly undertake this, with all of the anxiety over Bert's condition and the fact that I was with him most of each day and evening. However, true to my rigid rule, I made no protest and, under fairly harrowing circumstances, did what was necessary to sell the house, furnished. Thus, in January, 1968, I found myself living alone in a nudist park with no husband, no home, and five boxes of possessions in storage.

I had stayed on at the nudist park during the six months that Bert was in the hospital, helping with the breakfasts each morning and then leaving to drive the eight miles to the hospital for the rest of the day and evening. The owners and other members were kind, but it was a lonely and difficult time. Bert preferred not to have any visitors. My sister and her family in northern California did not know we were in the nudist park. I had written about Bert's surgery, explaining that we were trying to deal with his illness in accordance with the Religious Science ideas which see the mental attitude as an adjunct to and not a substitute for medicine. I said that it would be easier for me not to be trying to send conventional reports on his physical condition. Thus I was almost without any support from those close to me.

Bert's sufferings were appalling and it took all of our energy to deal with each crisis as it presented itself, almost constantly. The whole experience was so traumatic that for several years after Bert's death I could not even write the abbreviation for California—CA—on an envelope since it also said to me "Cancer."

The following summer I made plans for a long voyage alone, around the world, mostly by ship. Despite loneliness and some illness, a healing quality was in the experience. I was in a beautiful part of New Zealand on a sunny "summer" day on Christmas Eve, 1968, one year from the day of Bert's death. On the following day I was thinking back to "one year ago today," as I had probably done most of the three hundred and sixty-five days in between. But this day was different. This time, for the first time, it was true that I could not remember what I had done with Bert a year ago. This time, a year ago, he had been dead. This day was the beginning of the second year. A year ago I had been alone. Something important had been completed. Something new was ready to come in. I felt freed.

I thought about the ritual of a year of mourning, which I would have said was meaningless to me. But I discovered its meaning for me. That completed journey of the earth around the sun had permitted the completion in me of another kind of journey, and I was ready to move on.

The looking back which I had been doing all year had been full of pain; I still carried heavy feelings of guilt, for what I had done and not done "to Bert;" feelings that if somehow I'd known something more about healing he wouldn't have had to die. On that first day of the second year, when I could not look back to a year ago with Bert, it was as though the pain of the relationship eased and healed.

In the summer of 1969, after another illness in Greece, I returned to California and with helpful support from my family, arranged to make my home in Carmel, on the beautiful Monterey Peninsula south of San Francisco. Living alone in a tiny, rickety, charming one-room attic over an old red barn, I began a new life. My focus was on reconnecting with the essence of the 1929 experiences, which I believed to be universally meaningful for a human being. I actively, consciously, rekindled the central orientation of those earlier years. The focus was on the "spiritual," which I saw as the wholeness that integrates what we are, and relates it to all that is. As part of this I did some study of modern metaphysics and of Eastern mysticism, and experimented with forms of meditation.

Also I gave attention to the now well-accepted views of present-day psychology concerning our responsibility for our own feelings; and the fact that, in a profound sense, we "create our own reality." I could look back and see that Bert and I had really gone through most of thirty years of marriage without believing that each person is responsible for his or her own responses to what is going on. We had acted on our conditioned beliefs that either of us had the power to make the other happy or unhappy. We didn't see the way in which each was being a mirror for the other, a mirror which, had we known how to gaze into it and learn from it, could have taught us about our own possibilities for wholeness when we could embrace all the parts of ourselves, including those we had projected on the other person.

The later years revived an interest in parapsychology that had had its seeds in my undergraduate days as a psychology student when Dr. William McDougall came from England to Berkeley and told us his experiences with shell-shocked soldiers who, under hypnosis, recovered from hysterical paralysis and blindness. Many more ideas about the mind-body unity began to flower for me in the climate of the seventies. Associated with this was a growing interest in holistic health, which put me in touch with the work of Carl and Stephanie Simonton who were exploring psychological factors in the onset and treatment of cancer. Then, nearly eight years after Bert's death, I at last felt able to confront cancer once again.

In 1975, at age sixty-eight, after about twelve years of retirement, I decided to go back to work doing a special kind of spiritual or transpersonal psychotherapy with cancer patients. I was looking for a physician with whom I might work, who would have some understanding of the transformational process as I understood it. At that moment, I "happened" to attend a cancer conference in September 1975, near Los Angeles, where one of the speakers was a young internist of whom I had never heard. He worked with cancer patients but was now leaving his conventional practice of medicine to explore wider areas of consciousness, and energy fields of the human body.

This was Dr. Brugh Joy. In him I was astonished and delighted to discover a skilled physician with a specialty in internal medicine, a person who understood psychodynamics and psychotherapy, and one whose spiritual orientation included what I believed to be the essence of the transformational process. His own experiences of surrender had led him to remarkably expanded levels of consciousness and a willingness to share his explorations with others in groups.

I could scarcely believe that this was happening. Here, in one package, I seemed to be presented with everything— and more than everything—I had been asking for as I commenced a new kind of work with cancer patients.

During the next five years I had many opportunities to be close to Brugh Joy's work and his thought, which are described in his book *Joy's Way: A Map for the Transformational Journey, An Introduction to the Potentials for Healing with Body Energies* (Joy, 1978). My own numerous and varied experiences with Brugh opened whole new vistas of consciousness that had been inaccessible to me, which enriched my life and my work. Most of the new experiences involved the intuitive side, which had long been out of balance in me and was now being nourished.

Willingness to "open and allow" was the attitude that Brugh Joy encouraged in those who came to Sky Hi Ranch to participate in his residential conferences, usually of two weeks' duration, in the foothills of the San Bernardino mountains overlooking the high desert in California. A wide variety of experiences contributed to opening up access to intuitive knowing.

"Centering at heart level" was a phrase that epitomized Brugh's own discoveries before and after leaving the conventional practice of medicine. The centered state is the willingness state of non-attachment, of fluidity and flexibility to respond appropriately in the moment. The level of the heart symbolized Brugh's discoveries in working with the energy fields of the human body which he sensed and worked with in diseased or normal states, and of which the energy center in the mid-line of the body at the level of the heart appears to have a central importance. The level of the heart also symbolizes the paramount importance of a state that may be described as unconditional love. This state is not an emotion although it includes deep feeling. It is non-demanding, non-possessive, non-judgmental. It is a way of responding to all experience with an inclusive embrace. It can be thought of as an appreciation of and an appropriate, inclusive response to *what is*. In my terminology, unconditional love is the inevitable outcome of a single intention to allow the expression of WHATEVER is most inclusively harmonious and balanced, excluding nothing and no one.

In these last years, professional and personal relationships have deepened my understanding of the meaning of unconditional love. I am now ready to say that when such love issues from a balanced heart-level energy which recognizes the oneness of all forms, its power is transforming. Sometimes I can believe that it is the only power there is. To discover the meaning of unconditional love and embody it may then be the means for any real transformation in our collective life on this planet.

As I continued to encounter new experiences with Brugh Joy at Sky Hi Ranch and elsewhere, they felt to me like a great gift that could augment and enrich the strong foundation my life already had from the earlier years. They contributed to my personal growth and to the kind of psychotherapy I began to do with a few cancer patients, using discoveries Brugh had made in working with cancer. If persons facing cancer were ready to do so, I could sometimes help them look at the possibility that something within them might be sensing the need for a deep change in their lives, which looked impossible or too difficult to make. In consequence, some part of them might be wanting to die in order to bring about needed change.

Seeing cancer as a transformational disease opened an entirely new vista. If what the person was looking for was a deep change which would greatly improve the quality of life and make it really worth living, the focus could be on a

Big Change, not on fighting the cancer per se. The possibility then would exist, for the cancer patient as for anyone else, to seek fulfillment where it may be found—by wanting something that can be had, by substituting a single intention in place of numerous specific desires, including even the desire to be rid of the cancer. Many different factors affect the outcome of the disease process. My observation is that regardless of what changes occur in the physical body, the quality of life can be remarkably modified by a change in the person's basic inner orientation. I will say more about this in Chapter 19, "Toward Transformation through Cancer."

But first I need to tell you something more about my relationship with this young physician, Brugh Joy.

CHAPTER 11

A Personal Myth

To my own amazement I have endured within the last couple of years a period of anguish, despair, and fury that almost wiped me out before it taught me priceless lessons and carried me to a new level of steadiness and well-being. It was all part of my own transformational journey and I wrote it down for you to see.

However, I then realized that there was no way that you could understand the inwardness of what had happened to me unless I first told you about three personal experiences that I had never before written down. These separate episodes occurred over a period of nearly forty years and seemed unrelated, but they suddenly formed a pattern which profoundly influenced my life. If I am to give you my life, I must tell you these additional facts.

About a year after Bert and I were married, I became pregnant. That was an unalloyed disaster for us at the time. Bert was considered "totally and presumably permanently disabled" and was going to school part-time. I had a job earning $100 a month; we were living in a one-room furnished apartment in an old house with other people, where we shared a bath. How could we cope with a baby?

We had long discussions which got nowhere. Bert's first wife had had two pregnancies and two abortions. He saw no way whatever that a child could be part of our lives under the circumstances. He was distressed that our birth control precautions had not been effective, and could see no alternative to abortion.

I felt a deep conflict. I blamed myself for not having been careful enough about the contraceptive measures and I, too, saw no way that we could give proper care to a baby. Even if I were to go back to work after the birth, Bert certainly did not see himself in the role of permanent baby-sitter. He wanted to go on with his studies and he had begun to write some short stories, a craft which he hoped to perfect.

Within me was a deep sense of how "normal" this pregnancy seemed in my body and how profoundly I did not want to interrupt it. It represented a kind of completion and fulfillment of my beingness as a woman, and I welcomed it for that. But I saw no way to allow it to proceed.

I recall that Bert suggested that since I felt that way, I could give birth to the child and give it up for adoption. This felt to me intolerable. I was sure it would be even harder—much harder—than an abortion.

This was in the spring of 1938. Abortion was a word that was scarcely spoken aloud and certainly never in "polite society." I knew no one who had had one, and knew only the tales about the sordid, dirty, illegal places where such things were performed. Through a friend, Bert and I learned of a gynecologist who might be willing to perform the surgery in view of the nature of some of my recent maladies including a persistent kidney infection. This turned out to be true. The physician said that if we were serious about this, to protect my health, and if Bert would have a vasectomy, he would perform the operation in the local hospital. Bert was more than pleased to solve the matter in this way.

I continued to feel grave misgivings and a deep inward division. But we went ahead with the plan. The local hospital was Catholic, which made the whole experience seem even more alien and threatening. I was already feeling horribly guilty, but the nuns managed to make remarks about how such an operation as this should never be performed, and my sense of doing something dreadful continued to deepen.

When the surgeon had asked about my reactions to certain drugs, I had said that ether made me deathly sick, and he had replied that the anaesthetic would be gas. During the surgery, the supply of gas ran out and no reserve tank had been brought in. Therefore, I began to surface to consciousness. In that semi-conscious state, I either heard or imagined that I heard one of the nurse-nuns say sternly, "This is a terribly wicked thing that she is doing. It is really an unforgivable act." Then someone started the ether and I again lost consciousness. I vomited for three days after the surgery, and continued to hemorrhage for several weeks. The whole experience was a nightmare.

But I put it behind me, or thought I had. In fact, it was probably a few months later that Bert suggested the "open marriage," beginning with the Tanya episode and Kunkel's second circle of relationship. You have been through all of that with me in "The Middle Years."

Twenty years after the abortion (about which no one in my family ever knew for more than thirty years) I was in psychoanalysis. During the two previous years of graduate work at the University of Southern California, I had had excellent supervision for my work in clinical practice and I had learned a great deal about myself. I had seen how often my own inner blocks had blocked a client, and I had watched my manipulative tendencies get in the way of self-determination for the client. It was out of this, and the hope for improvement in the relationship with Bert, that I went into analysis when Bert and I decided to go on with our life together and I had moved back from Los Angeles.

My analytic sessions took place at eleven o'clock on Saturday mornings. One such morning near the end of the analysis I awoke from a powerful dream in which I gave birth to a beautiful, perfect, baby boy. My sense of fulfillment and joy and completion is indescribable. After twenty years it was the totally unexpected closing of a gestalt, or the final resolution of a long-held, unresolved chord of music. It was an ecstatically joyful and satisfying experience, culminating in the presence of this precious, perfect baby boy. I had my baby back at long last.

Sixteen more years passed before the next scene in this small, very personal drama. It was February 1976, and I was about to leave Carmel for my first visit to Sky Hi Ranch where I was to be one of sixteen men and women at a conference with Dr. Brugh Joy. There would be a fourteen-day intensive workshop followed by a third weekend together at the Ranch.

I had heard Brugh speak in September 1975 at the cancer conference I have mentioned. My going to that was in itself bizarre since I had had compelling reasons to be somewhere else that day, but had unhesitatingly cancelled those plans to attend the conference which offered five speakers, four of whom I knew or knew of. The fifth I had never heard of, W. Brugh Joy, M.D. Since I was looking for a physician who might be open to my ideas about working with cancer patients, it was inevitable that I would be immensely struck by the combination of qualities I sensed in Dr. Joy as I listened to his talk. Here in one person was the highly trained internist, wise psychotherapist and spiritually committed person. I could scarcely believe it.

At the end of that talk, he made his first public announcement of having leased Sky Hi Ranch, where he proposed, after the first of the year, to see some patients and to work with groups who might wish to explore with him some of the areas he was exploring. He invited any interested persons to get in touch with him.

This I did, with a great sense of expectancy. Following some correspondence he made telephone calls to invite the people who were to make up the groups in January, February and March 1976. To me he said, "I think your energies would fit best with the February group." I then got hold of a set of tapes of a presentation Brugh had made for the Center for the Healing Arts in July 1975, which gave details of his own development, including a remarkable, determinative meditation he had had which resulted in his decision at age thirty-five to leave a successful medical practice and to travel extensively, and which was followed by the complete disappearance of a recently-diagnosed serious and painful disease. These events and many others related to his discoveries about consciousness, energy fields of the human body, medicine and metaphysics, are now described in his book *Joy's Way* (Joy, 1978). However, at that time I had only the early tapes to which I listened with great interest and which I shared with friends.

The day before I was to leave for the Ranch, a friend called to say goodbye. "Now Fran," she said, "don't get carried away. Undoubtedly Dr. Joy is a remarkable young man but you have the knowledge and you are almost twice his age and are old enough to be his mother. So, enjoy—but don't get carried away." I laughed, thanked her for the advice and thought no more about it.

The events of the first couple of days in the group at the Ranch, in the starkly beautiful setting of snow-covered mountains and high desert, were enough to make me feel deeply moved by the extraordinary qualities which were apparent in Brugh and in his way of working. Before lunch on the third day, I walked a little way up the mountain and stood in the sharp, clear air looking across the desert to the far hills. All at once I thought, "My God, what if I *am* his mother?!"

The idea, of course, was related to my friend's comment and to the abortion and to my general impression of Brugh's age. I knew that his birthday was January 27th but I did not know the year. My abortion was in the spring of 1938.

I was amazed at the intensity of my own feelings as I wondered about this possible connection. Until not long before that time I had not even believed in reincarnation except in the vaguest terms of some kind of continuity of consciousness. But I had come to the Ranch because I felt open to allow myself to move to higher levels of consciousness, WHATEVER that might include. I felt a profound connection with Brugh because we shared the same foundation for our lives. The terminology differed somewhat but the core was our conviction about a centered committed state of openness and fluidity in following an inner direction.

Also there was the "coincidence" of his work with cancer and my own newly evolved plan to do psychotherapy with cancer patients, and my interest in finding a physician to work with. I knew that the form of his work, after leaving his traditional practice of medicine, had not yet taken shape, and that he was much interested in the place of group energies in the treatment of disease, and was exploring new ways of working from the basis of a surrendered, heart-level state of unconditional love. I began to think that my work might somehow link itself to his; I was free to work anywhere.

"What if," I thought, "after having 'killed' him, I am now being given a chance to serve him in his work in some way? Can it be that at last I can make up for what I did by joining my energies to his in a new and expanded way of working in this field where our deep interests come together?"

The possibility that this previous brief relationship might

have taken place was a tempting one, since it would provide an apparently then still-needed means of "righting a wrong" and would seem to explain why I had stumbled upon Brugh and his cancer work just as I was looking for ways to start mine. What I had felt to be acutely negative experiences would thus be balanced by this surprising new possibility that all of the parts of this story were connected as is everything else.

I knew that at the time of my pregnancy I was not ready to be a mother; I had had too many problems of my own to be able to nurture and allow to go free a child needing to develop his own potentialities. I also knew that Brugh's mother had apparently been exactly the one to nurture his development. But I was deeply moved by the possibility that, even briefly, that soul had been in my body, had then found its way to another mother, and was now, after highly scientific training, moving out into a whole new range of possibilities of the meaning of consciousness, and of healing. Brugh's mother had died unexpectedly in April 1975. I had come to Los Angeles and met him in September. And now we were here, at Sky Hi Ranch.

I walked down the mountain in a daze and encountered Brugh at the door of the dining-room.

"What year were you born?"

"1939."

"Oh, no!!"

At a later time I told Brugh this tale about the abortion, the dream, and my friend's remark on the eve of my coming to the Ranch. We talked about it then and we wrote and spoke about it in the months that followed. We were moved by numerous elements in our relationship which appeared to us to be synchronistic, meaningful coincidence. And the experiences in the February group at the Ranch strengthened a deep, loving connection between us.

Once a few months after my first visit to the Ranch I was in a quiet mood at home and found myself asking an "Inner

Knower," "What really is this business about a possible earlier mother-infant relationship between Brugh and me?" An answer came instantly, "You cannot possibly understand all that. Simply rest back and trust that there is a deep and meaningful connection between you two."

And Brugh and I know that this is true, WHATEVER form it may ever have taken or not taken. That does not matter. What matters is that each of us shall experience an expanding awareness of What Is, and shall allow all action to flow from that realization. There is a Work to be done —the expression of wholeness. I feel a deep connection with those everywhere, known and unknown to me, who live in wholehearted surrender to the expression of that Work, WHATEVER form it may take. And I know even more profoundly that that same potential is in every person, waiting for its awakening.

This feeling of oneness is unconditional love which is impersonal in its essence because it is universal. When I am in the centered, willingness state it is the kind of love I can feel for individuals, including Brugh.

However, I now realize that the vividness of my personal myth about the possible earlier relationship with Brugh, and my attachment to it, kept intensely alive in me an *emotion of conditional love* for Brugh. Countless times over the past few years, whether I was with Brugh or hundreds or thousands of miles away, I have fallen into (I almost wrote "wallowed in") an aching, poignant tenderness toward him, colored by a gentle, caring, protective concern associated with being a "tender mother." The emotion of *conditional* love always involves attachment. As you will see from what comes next, I still had a big lesson to learn in getting free from a conditional love which makes demands and has expectations, which asks to be special, which subtly attaches strings and wants something in return. If you don't believe that such conditional love can get you into trouble, move to the next chapter!

CHAPTER 12

The Oral Examination Trauma

THE MANY AND varied experiences of the later years pushed me into a growing conviction of the paramount importance of simplicity and clarity in answering the question, "How do we find a deep realization of the Self? What is the Source of our well-being and the fulfillment of our highest potential?" I believed that the answer was to want one thing, in the way I have been trying to describe. I saw the truth of this again and again in my own life, and in the lives of clients in therapy who were facing life-threatening diseases or life-stultifying problems and unfulfilling patterns. And I saw it in the people close to me with whom I shared the transformational journey.

About three years ago, all of this led me to feel that it was time for me to put onto paper what I had been learning for so long. If it was as essentially simple as I thought it was, surely I could make it clear to anyone who had an open mind and an urge for the most that life could offer, individually and collectively. So I decided to write a small, simple, clear "How To" book.

Not long after starting work on this, I revived an interest I had dropped years before, to complete a Ph.D. degree. I knew that the general subject matter was suitable for a doctoral dissertation in counseling psychology, which would mean that much of the same material which I would use in the dissertation could be used later in the book. So, I undertook to complete the other requirements for the degree, and then went to work on the dissertation.

The chairman of my Ph.D. committee, Dr. Michael Cohen, discussed with me the make-up of the committee. Dr. Paul Brenner was an obvious choice since he was a member of the faculty who knew me and had some knowledge of my work. Dr. Cohen then suggested that the other committee member might be Dr. Brugh Joy. He was aware that I had participated in a number of groups with Dr. Joy for several years. I thought that Brugh's presence on the committee would be entirely suitable in view of our mutual interest in the transformational process. I foresaw no difficulty, and in fact "assumed" that Brugh's understanding and appreciation of my views and of my psychotherapeutic work would be the equivalent of his approval of the dissertation. That unquestioning certainty about what I could expect from Paul Brenner's and Brugh Joy's presence on the committee led straight into the nightmare that later engulfed me at the oral examination.

In the meantime, early in my work on the dissertation, I spent a long weekend in February 1979 at one of Brugh's conferences at Sky Hi Ranch with a group of people who had attended previous two-week conferences. During one of the group sessions, Brugh took the occasion to point out to me some attitudes of mine that he believed needed to be looked at. In each case they represented a tendency to be skewed to the positive side, the "light" side, with an effort to change something that was seen to need "healing" in a specific way. I knew without any question that Brugh's comments were offered out of a concern for my growth and a belief in my potential for growth, and out of a conviction that I was close to important new insights but not quite there. He said as much in the group.

However, to my own amazement, I found myself intensely angry with him and resentful at his not being able to help me see exactly what he was trying to tell me. I felt that not only was he pointing out my limitations "in front of God and everybody," but that he was also not making at all clear to me just what he thought I was doing that required correction, for balance. Although I was one of those who had been associated with his work almost from the beginning, it now felt as if I were publicly flunking some sort of test.

Later that night my anger and frustration and sense of defeat deepened, and in bed I was crying and saying to myself, "This path is too hard; it's too hard." In the morning I had time for a long meditation, and in the final session I shared with the group some of what my feelings had been. Interestingly, I brought up all sorts of resentments that I had felt against Brugh for a long time, but had never faced or voiced. I managed to tell most of this tale with humor, so that all of us, including Brugh, were shouting with laughter over the anger at him that I was dredging up. As I talked, resentments came out of me that I had no realization of having felt. They had been buried under the surface and had been rumbling in the depths without any previous recognition by me of how angry I was at some of Brugh's previous actions in relation to me.

As an example, I said, "You know how Brugh talks about getting away from rigidity, and rigid, conditioned patterns of response. He has mentioned the rigidity of people who compulsively write Thank You notes. Well, I am feeling that that's one piece of rigidity that he could use a little more of!!'' (Loud laughter from Brugh, from me, and from the group). Part of their hilarious laughter came from some of their own experiences of not always getting from Brugh a particular response they were expecting. Part came from their deep admiration for Brugh as a teacher, but also from their sense of identification with a fellow group member who had the temerity to confront him in a way they might have liked to do.

Then I continued, "Here I am, in Europe for instance, going to meetings on alternative treatment methods and holistic health, and sending Brugh all kinds of fascinating, interesting items I run across which will help him in his work. And what do I hear from him? Not one living word!!''

Again, much laughter, but through all of my comments there was still a real edge of resentment. Obviously I had wanted particular sorts of response to my "loving, thoughtful" acts, and they hadn't been forthcoming in the particular forms I was unconsciously demanding. Of course, this is not to say that Brugh was recommending that one never express appreciation. He can and does do that, abundantly. But that has nothing to do with whether I am in a fluid, willingness state or whether, on the contrary, my giving and loving is conditional, with strings attached.

That morning I was still not fully allowing myself to face the anger and resentment I felt toward Brugh. This was, of course, made more difficult since I simultaneously was feeling for him a profound love and appreciation because of all of our shared experiences in the previous years, and because of the special tenderness I felt for him in view of my "personal myth."

I was also unable to grasp what he meant by his effort to have me look at a one-sidedness in myself, a lack of wholeness which expressed in my being primarily on the "light" side, the positive side, the side of the "best." Actually, of course, the emergence of some of these negative emotions and my discomfort with them were essential steps toward my having to face them eventually as part of my wholeness, my personal collective. Although I didn't know it, that process was well under way and, in early October at the oral examination on the dissertation it was going to wipe me out into nothing before I would "get it all together," embracing my wholeness to the point where I could understand what Brugh had said to me in February.

In the months between, while I was still stumbling along doing my best to understand the balance that Brugh was suggesting I needed, I worked hard on the dissertation. The members of the committee knew my views on the transformational process and were in general touch with my progress. However, practical considerations kept to a minimum their opportunities to see the dissertation during its writing, until it was submitted to each of them before the oral examination.

I was concurrently preparing the manuscript for a book to be based on the same work and I was "wanting" to complete the doctorate before publication of the book. To facilitate this, and because I felt so sure of the validity of the work, I had even gone to the expense and the risk of having the dissertation typed in final form before the oral examination!

The day before, I sat myself down and told myself that I didn't "want" the approval of the committee; I didn't "want" the degree; and in particular I didn't "want" the degree before the publication of the book. I said that what I wanted was to allow WHATEVER was appropriate in the circumstances; I wanted to flow with WHATEVER was most inclusive and whole. Goodness knows I was trying to want only that, but I was attached.

The result was that the oral examination was one of the most grueling experiences of my life. Although they were appreciative of parts of the work, all of the members of the committee asked for changes. All said that it was essential for me to include more of my own personal journey. In the original version I told of the two canoe experiences, but gave nothing more about my own life, except as it could be inferred by my enthusiastic explanations about the wonders of living by the transformational process. All of the fifty years between age twenty-two and seventy-two were missing. The committee stressed that the kind of "bare bones" quintessential descriptions I had given of substituting one single intention for all specific desires simply did not communicate what I was wanting to convey.

This was bad enough, since it would require radical revision, delay, and re-typing. Worse than this was the criticism of fundamental internal inconsistencies. All of the members pointed these out, but, because of my earlier history with Brugh, his "sword thrusts" were the ones that slashed me to bits. He said that I was affirming that one needed to embrace the totality, but that I then denied this by using terms like "best" or "right" in what appeared to be a restrictive sense which excluded parts of reality rather than embracing them in a larger whole. He saw this tendency in some of my comments on individual human development and also on large social and political movements at work on the planet. He said that I was failing to see the place and function of destruction and chaos as part of an on-going totality. He stressed that the members of the committee were not trying to write my dissertation for me but that they had a responsibility to ask for internal consistency. He found this lacking, and had marked numerous examples of what he considered to be conditioned value judgments which invalidated my major position.

I defended myself as best I could when I believed his comments were unjustified, and I attempted to get clarification for the points I could not understand. But it was a totally unexpected turn of events which felt like an onslaught, an attack of some cherished convictions. Most painful was the feeling, as the session wore on, that the strong, solid foundation of basic agreement which I had always felt with Brugh was slithering away like quicksilver. Many of his comments, written and oral, were so fundamentally challenging that they seemed to negate some of my most basic understandings, and to wipe out the main value which I believed was in the dissertation. I could not believe what I was seeing and hearing from him.

The members of the committee all indicated the changes they would like to see, and tried to make these seem minimal. To me they sounded monumental. In the end, despite much that was said appreciatively to the contrary, I felt wiped out, set at naught, worthless. This was clearly because of the assumption I had made that the committee would view the work essentially as I saw it, and would find it entirely acceptable. To this picture of how things "should" be, I was obviously attached. I had been attached to what I had written, attached to completing the degree before publication of the book, attached to receiving the approval of the committee that day.

When the others had gone and I was left alone for a time, I began to let myself experience what I was really feeling, which was that I was furiously, murderously angry, particularly at Brugh. I had not felt that much anger in a long, long time. This was some of my own deeply negative feeling that I surely had not been owning as part of myself. Now it felt like a powerful force and I gave it full sway.

A close friend who is a therapist, Edith Sullwold, came after the examination to "celebrate" with me. Instead, we listened to a tape of the session. She told me that the fact was that the comments had not been as devastating as I had experienced them and therefore she suggested that I should look back at my life to other occasions when I had had similar feelings of being wiped out and made into nothing. She believed that getting in touch with that pattern would "unhook" me from the particular hurt and anger of the oral examination.

And that is what I did. I took a week and spent it in Hemet with Gertrude Karnow, another close friend who is a therapist and who took on this healing task with me. We used dreams, waking dreams, and active imagination in connection with past events through the years. I re-experienced the dream of giving birth to the baby boy twenty years after the abortion, and this time I myself cut the cord. Also, we went through the dissertation session in detail, with my re-living the *real* feelings I had had but had swallowed. Then I dealt with what I had swallowed! The whole time was immensely revelatory and helpful. I fully experienced the hurt and the rage and the sense of bewilderment and betrayal.

During the hours that I was alone in the car driving back to Carmel, I was still shouting at Brugh, "How could you do this to *me?* How *could* you? How can you tear apart this truth that I have written? Who are you to question these things I have said, which come out of a deep knowledge and experience? Now I see that we don't even have the same basic view of life. You are somewhere that I don't want to be. I don't care if I never see you again!"

Later when I talked by phone with Edith Sullwold I said, "You would have been proud of me. I was yelling at Brugh all the way home." She laughed and agreed that it was essential for me to be in touch with the negative feelings, which in the past I had so steadfastly kept hidden from myself. But she went on, "However, it is equally important for you to recognize that the anger is misplaced. The anger is not directed at Brugh but at yourself—at the Frances you have never fully accepted as a worthy, whole being."

I told her that when I arrived home I had found a long letter from Brugh, expressing understanding of the "sting" of the oral examination, and hoping that I was able to view it now from a wider perspective in which I could see how much the dissertation contained which was valid and usable. He went on to try to explain to me again in various ways the essential point he had made during the session about the necessity for inclusiveness of all the opposites. A couple of the passages in his letter still made me furious and were incomprehensible to me. I read one of these to Edith and demanded, "Can you make any sense out of that?" She was silent for a moment and then replied, "Yes, I can. And I think that when all the hurt and the anger are gone, you also will understand what he is saying to you."

Some five weeks after the oral examination I had an impulse to call Brugh. Working through the hate and the anger had indeed made me able to see more clearly what he had been trying to point out to me about the inconsistencies. I felt ready to talk with him again. We had a long, full interchange, which we both appreciated. We spoke of my unrecognized anger which had flared out at him for what he had said to me in the February group at Sky Hi Ranch, and the even more devastating hurt and fury and hate which had surfaced in me as a result of his criticism of what he saw as vital inconsistencies in the dissertation. Because of what he had said in the oral examination session, my wounds and anger and bewilderment had been so intense that it was a couple of weeks before I could even bring myself to look at the scores of written comments (some of them highly favorable) which he had sprinkled liberally on his copy of the dissertation, and which he had offered to me.

Brugh had been fully aware of the effect which his sword thrusts might have on me. He said, "It would have been so much easier just to let it go, and not raise the troublesome questions. But you were so close, and I believed you could take that next step to include it all. It was a way to bring you back into the overview."

I told him how that morning I had watched on television while the Iranian students who had just recently taken the American hostages were describing their murderous rage against the former Shah for what he had done to their fellow-students and their families and friends. I said, "I could understand them perfectly, because it was exactly the same murderous rage I've been feeling against you!" Brugh was delighted, saying that he could tell by my voice that there had been a real resolution to what I had been going through.

And I think we both recognized deeply, without words, that we knew the simple answer to my screaming query as I was driving alone in the car. The question is, "How could you *do* this to *me?*" And the answer is "Unconditional love."

At a later time I spent several days with Jeannette Hedge, a friend who is a past-life therapist, in my effort to go as deeply as I could into the roots of this old pattern. One segment of the material that surfaced in my psyche had to do with a series of episodes in which I was the helpless victim. In another series of episodes I was the powerful, cruel tyrant. These were not at all experienced by me as "former lives" with which I had any sense of connection or memory. Rather, they were bits of drama which vividly and emotionally presented the feelings connected with these two diametrically opposite states. Later, out of these opposites, there emerged some images that symbolized a balanced, centered state in which all options were open to me, allowing the choice of whatever the situation called for. The effect was profoundly healing.

Having done some work on myself, I felt ready to return to the dissertation, to see what I could do to meet the committee's suggestions, which I could by then accept as valid. I had not yet written any of the additional autobiographical material, and I did not see how I was going to fit it in with the main body of the work I had already done. I had set a self-imposed deadline for completing certain work and was beginning to feel the pressure.

At that point one of my friends who is exceptionally

forthright and honest asked me some penetrating questions about what I was doing. Was I caught in the need to achieve some goals? Did I have some sort of time-table for getting these goals accomplished? Was I trying to "engineer" anything? Or was I letting each day, each moment, tell me what it required of me?

Of course, these were not new questions, but I took some quiet time alone to look at them. I asked myself, "Would you really be *willing* to abandon the whole Ph.D. effort and view it simply as one of the possible options open to you?" That was a hard one. I found myself remembering back to the second canoe experience, in which I realized that the only question for me to answer was, "Am I willing?" Now, in the present moment I had to keep stopping myself from thinking about the situation logically, rationally, weighing pros and cons of completing the Ph.D. or dropping the whole project. I was continuing to list mentally all of the probable advantages to my doggedly completing the work.

But a part of me with which I think we are all endowed was saying, "None of these considerations has anything whatever to do with the question. The question is, 'Would you be *willing* to drop the whole thing?' " Answering this question demanded of me that I answer these other questions: "What do you really live by? What is the Source of your nourishment? What matters to you more than anything else? What gives you fulfillment and a sense of well-being? What is the one thing for which you would give up everything else?"

And the answer to all of these is, "Being willing to open and allow the expression of WHATEVER is appropriate to the whole situation." When I am at this level of consciousness I know that any other attitude, any holding on, is intolerable; I know that no specific attachment, no matter how appealing to some part of me, can match the feeling that accompanies that wholehearted state of willingness in which I am "in the flow" and am nourished by a feeling of connection and oneness with a vast whole of which I am a part (in the sense of the drop in the ocean) and which I am consciously choosing to express, no matter what may be called for.

That is what feeds me; that is what gives me deep satisfaction and a sense of my own wholeness. That is the state I choose, when I am willing to listen to the direction of the inner core of me, which is my Self. For me, that is Self-fulfillment, and nothing else is.

So—what did the oral examination experience do for me? It forced me to listen to an inner demand to face my own negativity, and to embrace parts of myself that I had repressed and denied. I had to own the raging fury and hatred I had been feeling against someone I deeply loved. And I had to embrace the "non-acceptable Frances." For the person I was, at seventy-two, that was profoundly unsettling!

Also, the experience pushed me into wrestling with the larger issues I was dealing with in the dissertation. Did I know what wholeness meant or was I still subtly refusing to look at destruction, separation, pain, and death as part of wholeness? Could I include all in the all, or was I still excluding parts? Did I see a universe or a duo-verse? Is there One or is there a duality? Can all mean *all?*

The pain involved in the totally unexpected frustration of my "wants" to have the dissertation accepted was itself the force to drive me, first into the rage and finally into the resolution at a very deep level from which I could re-write the dissertation in acceptable form. I would not choose to re-experience all that that examination session brought to me. But it was invaluable, and essential to my owning more of my own wholeness. For that I am honestly and profoundly grateful.

In a more personal way, I am fully aware that the intensity of the pain in the examination experience came from the nature of my relationship to Brugh over the years, and in particular from my attachment to the "personal myth." In the process of writing down and pondering the details of those apparently synchronistic events, I am experiencing my inner growth continuing to go on.

For I now have the feeling that all that has happened has in some way simply been part of the big and ever-repeated life-lesson concerning the limitations we impose upon ourselves by attachment and by conditional love. The fact is that over the years I have met a series of circumstances and have done with them as best I could at the time. I can accept and "forgive" myself.

Still dimly but more clearly now, I feel the synchronicity of these events as parts of my developing wholeness, but without the need to delineate them as steps in a particular relationship. I now feel more able than ever before to surrender even the "specialness" of a particular tenderness for Brugh because of an association with a lost baby. Another subtle level of attachment has slipped away; I do not feel the same need of it now.

In its place I have an image of Kuan Yin, the Chinese goddess of mercy, whose compassionate arms reach out equally to all, excluding no one.

CHAPTER 13

Embracing My Own Wholeness

"MY WHOLENESS, WHATEVER that may be, belongs to The Wholeness WHATEVER that may be." This is my present way of stating the transformational process. It has grown out of my willingness to go back over the events of my life and to remove the labels I previously placed on each segment of experience. There are the episodes I used to characterize as terrible, awful, intolerable, shameful, bad; and there are those I labeled as beautiful, wonderful, ecstatic, good.

With greater wisdom I ask myself, "What have you accomplished when you place a label on an experience?" In answering I can see that whether I call something bad or good, the simple fact remains that I still must give an appropriate response to the situation, WHATEVER it may be. To put on a label is to obscure WHAT IS. It clouds my view and limits my possibilities of response because I have limited my view of reality.

You can see how this has worked in the examples I have given you of episodes in my life. I would have said that two of the worst, most destructive, most devastating were the early ones: the story of the bellowed announcement on the pier, "It's a girl!" and the shrill pronouncement by the teacher, "You're a cheat!" The shame, humiliation, despair, and rejection as an outcast were laid down deep in my psyche in a way which colored my whole life. And yet these experiences clearly served to force me, eventually, to face myself squarely and honestly and to look at what I really am and to accept and embrace it all. This is liberation.

Similarly, the childhood accident forced a shift from being a conventionally pretty young girl into being something other than that, with different values which led me far and deep. The accident, and the near-fatal illness during my senior year in college, left me with a vague but persistent feeling that twice my life had apparently been saved for "something."

In the episode of my fiancé's declaring that he loved my best friend, not me, two narrow and possessive relationships were suddenly torn away from me and I was left abandoned, cast into total darkness. Serious illnesses and some surgery followed this, and once more flattened me into a time of enforced change, and new perspectives.

The trauma of Bert and Tanya was prolonged and intensely painful. To try to hold on to Bert's love I had to be willing to violate something deep within me which said, "I can't bear it." But as the lesser of two "evils" I chose to bear it, and the ensuing years of the open marriage provided experience in my fruitless efforts to cope with desires that could not be satisfied at the level of particular desires and attachments. Neither the marriage nor the extra-marital affairs were fulfilling. And it was only rarely that I could move to a level above the problem, where my freedom and fulfillment came from my willingness to allow WHATEVER.

Now that I can look back and feel into a long lifetime, I know that every one of the experiences has had an essential meaning for my wholeness. Without them I would not be what I am now and what I have it in me to become. I needed every one of the lessons for my growth as an integrated Self.

They have acted as fires to force me to move out of the depths I have fallen into; they have proved to me again and again and again and again (Will it never end? No!) that the way of attachment closes off the multiple, creative options which wholeness offers to me, and to humanity. The devastating experiences emptied me into a nothing so that I could contain everything.

These rejections and desperations and agonies have bludgeoned me into an answer to those other questions I was asking myself, "What do you really live by? What is the Source of your nourishment? What gives you fulfillment and a sense of well-being?" The answer is the unconditional, self-chosen willingness state in which I can rest at my center, while all of my energies—physical, emotional, intellectual, and spiritual—are integrated and ready for WHATEVER expression is appropriate to wholeness.

Our path as human beings seems always to lead us first into the state of separateness, where we experience ourselves as alone, vulnerable, and fearful of attack. Our deliverance from this restricted state is our recognition of the oneness of all things. We experience ourselves as part of a limitless wholeness, of which everyone and everything is a part. Thus, to "lose my life" is to find my Life. There is no loss, no sacrifice. "My wholeness, WHATEVER that may be, belongs to The Wholeness, WHATEVER that my be." In this I am fulfilled.

CHAPTER 14

Knowledge of What to Do

W HEN I WAS twenty one, on that first trip around the world, I found myself late one afternoon on a train in Japan. For about six months I had been traveling from west to east, by ship and by train, having finally left China by way of Manchuria and Korea and Japan. By that time I was feeling homesick for California and as the ocean began to appear on the right side of the train as it traveled north I thought, "Ah, at last I will once again see the sun set over the Pacific Ocean, as I have seen it hundreds of times in San Francisco."

But to my utter consternation, the sun was setting on the left side of the train behind the mountains to the west. My world was turned upside down. How could it be that I was once again on the shores of the Pacific Ocean but the sun was setting, not into the ocean but behind the mountains?

During the long journey, I had often thought deeply about students all over the world, and about the essential oneness of all mankind, despite enormous differences and divisions. Even then, the ties which unite us seemed much more significant to me than the chasms which divided us.

So I thought, "What if a student from Japan and a student from California should be in the midst of an argument? The student from California would say, "I know that the sun sets in the Pacific Ocean. I see it every day." And the student from Japan would say, "But I *know* that the sun rises in the Pacific Ocean; I see it every day." And someone high above the Hawaiian Islands would say, "You are both right; the sun both rises and sets in the Pacific Ocean."

It occurs to me now that a far more exciting answer comes to us today from astronauts like Edgar Mitchell and Russell Schweickart, who have seen with their eyes what Copernicus knew with the genius of his mind. They can as easily say, "No, you are both wrong. The sun neither rises nor sets in the Pacific Ocean. That ocean is simply a patch of blue on a tiny planet which turns daily on its own axis as it moves slowly around the sun, the source of its life, year by year. That planet is a wholeness, and as we view it from space it has no frontiers, no borders, no dividing lines."

Today I am profoundly struck by the realization that we are participating in the birth of a New Age as revolutionary as the one glimpsed by Copernicus. Countless elements are coming together, from microbiology, subatomic physics, astronomy, medicine, transpersonal psychology, philosophy, and religion, to open our eyes to what we really are and to what we have in us to become.

The transformational process as I describe it is a simplified statement of the deepest wisdom of mankind. It has

always been true; it always will be true, but today we have
access to it in a manner never before possible. This is happening under many influences, some of which we can see
and others of which are only beginning to be discernible to
the most open minds and spirits among us.

This memory of my sunset experience in Japan has illuminated for me something of the nature of the difficulty
experienced by a human being who would like to open to
more of what life may have to offer, and who is given an
explanation, such as this, of the transformational process
of self-realization. He is enmeshed in the concrete details
of his life. He has to make a living, one way or another. He
wants security and comfort. He wants freedom from fear.
He wants peace; he wants excitement. He wants close relationships; he wants no ties. He wants to be treated as he
thinks he ought to be treated by others and by destiny; he
wants!

When I say to such a person, "Want only one thing—
WHATEVER expresses wholeness," he must say to me,
"But how on earth will I know what expresses wholeness?
And what if this is happening? What if that is happening?
What if 'they' are doing this to me?"

Of course these are all sensible, obvious, natural
questions when one asks them from the perspective of the
uncentered self. And the difficulty is that they can never be
satisfactorily answered as long as one remains within that
perspective, attached to specifics and asking about specific
future actions.

Perhaps you as the reader can imagine yourself in the
position of the person I have been describing. You hear for
the first time this suggestion for centering and unifying
yourself by wanting one thing only. But, without having
done that, you immediately begin to ask yourself a lot of

questions about how you will possibly be able to know this or that, and how you will act in this or that particular instance involving this or that complicated problem and this or that "impossible" person. My injunction for you here is quite simple: "STOP IT!"

Unless and until you have made the choice to try, even as a serious experiment, the condition required by the transformational process, which moves you into a different level of consciousness, you will never be able to answer these questions except from the level of the uncentered self, the fragmented, conflicted, attached, frustrated being we all are unless we make the one great change in our direction.

While you are saying, "Yes, but . . . how could it possibly work in this case of mine?" you are still caught in the problem and haven't yet done what is required to move to the perspective from which you have access to the resolution of the problem.

This isn't primarily a process about what to *Do* in specific situations. It is first and foremost a process about how to *BE* in a certain inner state, regardless of the specific situation. *BEING* in this state of willingness, by wanting only the one thing, is what gives you the ability to *DO* what each situation needs from you, and to know what that is.

Willingness allows us to see. From a higher, detached perspective, we can then know what to do. We are not insisting on going in any particular way, nor are we refusing to go in any particular way. We are willing to go in any way which represents our most inclusive view of reality which, in advance and in general, we have freely and fully chosen to express in our lives. We are willing to entertain any possibility, in order to express the one which fits the situation as it *is,* not as we wish it were.

One may describe all of this as a shift in levels of consciousness, which it is. This single intention or will to allow WHATEVER expresses wholeness, places us in a totally new and different state of consciousness from that which we occupy when we are at the level where we are attached to specifics, and are demanding particular outcomes. Most people have no conception of what state they would be in if they did let go of attachments to specific things. For this reason, they cannot conceive of how natural it would be, in this detached, fluid state of willingness, to see what the appropriate response would be, moment by moment. So they keep asking, "How will I know what to do?"

The idea of shifting to another level of consciousness may be an easy concept for some. For others, it may be more helpful to think simply of a conscious inner act, to change the object of what one wants. They are the same thing. It's the shift in consciousness from wanting a myriad of separate things, persons, events, to wanting only to respond appropriately in the moment.

This shift in our inner attitude allows us access to an intuitive knowing. We give it freedom to speak clearly to us when all that we want is to hear what it has to say to us, and to act accordingly. By this attunement to an inner knowledge, we are in touch with the Source of all we need to know.

If we are still asking, "What is the appropriate response?" the simplest answer is that it is WHATEVER we see to do when we have let go of the specifics, when we are not holding on to narrow, personality-level attachments. It is what offers itself to us as an answer when we are truly open to allow WHATEVER wants to express through us in the creative moment, to fulfill our highest potential.

If we decide to meet the requirement for *Being* in the willingness state, even with an experimental approach, we can allow our resultant experiences to confirm or negate our hypothesis. This can be a kind of trust, for the purposes of the experiment. I can trust that there may be an appropriate action which I can see if I am wanting only to perform that action when I see it, WHATEVER it may be. I can trust that "something wants to happen." I can trust that if I choose to express wholeness, I will be led into specific, concrete action which is appropriate for me and for others. I can trust that each moment does "call for something" from me, and that my openness to it will allow me to see what it is.

When we make this choice, experimentally but wholeheartedly, we have moved to another level of consciousness. We are at a level which is above the struggle, above the specific problem. The higher perspective which is provided by the single intention illuminates what was the struggle and what was the problem. In this new light, with detachment from specifics and attachment only to WHATEVER is inclusively appropriate, answers begin to present themselves to us moment by moment.

If I am centered and open to any option, I have at my disposal a limitless wisdom which includes the capacities of the intuitive, right hemisphere of my brain; and my linear, rational, left cerebral hemisphere; and as much experience as I dare to claim as being accessible to me, from my "own" conscious and unconscious mind, the collective unconscious of the race, and a universal superconscious mind such as Barbara Brown discusses in *Supermind: The Ultimate Energy* (Brown, 1980). Mystics for thousands of years have had access to a cosmic consciousness.

Even with all of these staggering possibilities of information and direction for our responses, we may still find that our actual experience much of the time is that we center ourselves in the non-attached willingness state, and then trust. We are often not really sure, but at some point when we have done all we know to do to be honestly willing and ready to respond appropriately . . . WHATEVER, and have used our rational minds as far as they go, we simply trust an inner prompting. Following that, we can observe the results of our action and gain further experience to teach us something more for the next time.

Our growing awareness of the nature of consciousness makes it easier to understand that the information necessary for appropriate action is available to us. On my desk are seven books that I have just been reading or re-reading. They are: Edgar Mitchell's *Psychic Exploration: A Challenge to Science* (Mitchell & White, Eds., 1974); Brugh Joy's *Joy's Way: A Map for the Transformational Journey, An Introduction to the Potentials for Healing with Body Energies* (Joy, 1978); Barbara Brown's *Supermind: The Ultimate Energy* (Brown, 1980); Marilyn Ferguson's *The Aquarian Conspiracy: Personal and Social Transformation in the 1980's* (Ferguson, 1980); Frances Vaughan's *Awakening Intuition* (Vaughan, 1979); Jean Shinoda Bolen's *The Tao of Psychology: Synchronicity and the Self* (Bolen, 1979); and Satprem's *Sri Aurobindo, or the Adventure of Consciousness* (Satprem, 1968).

As I open my mind to interact with these ideas and these experiences, I clearly feel myself, and the human species, to be part of a vast evolutionary movement. And the uniqueness of the present moment is that we are beginning to see that if we choose, we may consciously cooperate with the unfolding of this evolutionary movement.

These books that I have mentioned are among many which deal with evidence gathered from a wide variety of sources to show that minds are joined, and that consciousness is apparently limitless, and that everything is interrelated in a wholeness of energy / consciousness.

I shall not make the attempt to describe the concept of the hologram, except to say that it is a special method of photography which produces a three-dimensional image on a film. To me its most striking feature is that the whole image of the object photographed is present everywhere on the film, no matter how small a segment is cut out. The entire image is found on every piece.

Important research is now in progress on the hypothesis

that the brain itself may be like a hologram. Dr. Karl Pribram, a neurophysiologist, finds evidence for a holographic model of the brain, both from the physical structure of the brain and from its modes of functioning.

Others have commented on the relevance of this to our question about the availability to each one of us of vast areas of knowledge existing in consciousness. Brugh Joy has written, "If our own holographic negative contains the totality of awareness, we can have access to anybody's thought—past, present or future" (Joy, 1978).

George Leonard, in his enchantingly beautiful book, *The Silent Pulse,* concludes a clear description of the hologram with this, "In such a universe, information about the whole of it is available—at its every point. . . . All possible knowledge, in its general outlines if not in its sharply focused particulars, is potentially available to you, not just knowledge of the present, but of the past and of at least some of the future" (Leonard, 1978).

How does all of this relate to wanting one thing? My purpose in writing this book is to point out that the basic condition for the availability to an individual of all of this information is to want one thing, namely, to open to the available information as expansively as possible, and to allow it to direct one's life.

A practical result of being the centered, integrated Self is the experience of gathering together what we are in such a way that all of our capacities and energies are available to us at any time at their appropriate levels—physical, emotional, intellectual, spiritual. These energies are not imperious or separate. They are integrated by being ready for WHATEVER response our expanding view of the total situation calls for.

My own experience and observation is that many of our difficulties arise because we continue, again and again and again, to reverse the order in which we ask ourselves two vital questions: "What shall I *DO* in this situation?"—and —"Am I *BEING* centered in the willingness state?" The uncentered self asks first, "What shall I *do?*" The centered Self asks first, "Am I *being willing* to do or not to do any of the multiple potential actions available to me?"

It may be simplistic, but I am inclined to say that our sense of well-being and fulfillment is crucially affected by which question we address first. While we are asking, "What shall I do?" we are at a level of consciousness dealing with specific problems to which we have attachments and aversions which limit and distort our view. While we are asking, "Am I *being willing?*" we are at a different level of consciousness in which we are opening to any possibility. This *being willing* opens us up to WHATEVER knowledge and information and wisdom are available "anywhere" to direct our actions. We are asking wholeness to express as us. With an even deeper identification we can say that *we are being wholeness* in expression. Wholeness is not "out there." A fusion is experienced.

When we choose first to BE in the centered willingness state, our response in each situation flows effortlessly and wholeheartedly into appropriate action, the DOING. We are not bringing with us a pre-determined "should" or "should not" about how to respond, nor a specific desire nor aversion. All that we bring to each moment is a centered Self, voluntarily committed in advance to wholeness and inclusiveness.

The will has done its only work; it has wanted the one thing. Now our whole Self can move freely, without conflict, strain, effort, resistance, or frustration, into WHATEVER action fits the moment. Knowledge is thus available to us and permits an unimpeded flow of energy in wholehearted action. Such action utilizes whatever parts of us, whatever sub-personalities, whatever energies are appropriate to the action.

CHAPTER 15

Value Judgments and
Decision Making

WE HAVE BEEN considering the way in which the centered Self emerges as we want one thing. We have seen how the knowledge of what to do is implicit in the undefined commitment we have made, in advance of any specific circumstance which requires action.

Now we will examine successively four areas in which the centered Self finds itself functioning in daily life. I am saying "finds itself functioning" because my own experience and that of friends and clients is that the actions in these four areas seem to flow naturally from the centered willingness state. They are not "moral imperatives"; they are not external "shoulds" or "oughts." They are the Doing which seems often to come spontaneously from an inner state of Being. They are wholeness expressing in action. The four areas I will describe are: value judgments and decision making; acceptance of others and of ourselves;

forgiveness; and unconditional love. We will look at them in turn.

In going back over the events in my life which seemed "good" or "bad," we have been able to see the futility of putting value judgments on personal experiences. That futility is magnified when we realize how we distort reality when we insist upon placing value judgments on people and things around us, whether or not they seem to touch our lives directly.

In ordinary states of consciousness, when we are not centered in the state of willingness . . . WHATEVER, we perceive everything through a veil of our past conditioning, our opinions, our "ideas about," our emotions, desires, addictions, preferences, dislikes, and aversions. Unless we are maintaining the single intention to relate to What Is, it is impossible to perceive things and people without imposing value judgments that distort our view.

The integrated Self which forms this generalized attunement begins to learn to look at things and people *as they are*. This is extraordinarily rare. Nearly always we approach things with our vision blurred by past conditioning and by value judgments. We already have in our minds, for example, how people "ought" to look under certain circumstances, how we would "like" to have them act, what is "intolerable" behavior and what is "acceptable" behavior, in our view. And usually we don't even think of it as "our" view; we believe that it is "the" view. That kind of view can get so blurred that we have no chance to see the person or the situation that is really there. And we do it all the time. The result is that our actions and our decisions are distorted and erroneous because they are based on an unreal picture of what is going on.

I know of no more striking presentation of this matter of perception without value judgments than that of Rudolf Steiner. He wrote:

One of the first qualities that everyone wishing to acquire a vision of higher facts has to develop . . . is the unreserved, unprejudiced laying of oneself open to what is revealed by human life or by the world external to man. If a man approaches a fact in the world around him with a judgment arising from his life up to the present, he shuts himself off by this judgment from the quiet, complete effect that the fact can have on him. The learner must be able each moment to make of himself a perfectly empty vessel into which the new world flows. Knowledge is received only in those moments in which every judgment, every criticism coming from ourselves, is silent. . . .

Complete inner selflessness is necessary for this yielding of oneself up to the revelations of the new world. . . . Anyone who wishes to tread the path of higher knowledge must train himself to be able at any given moment to obliterate himself with all his prejudices. As long as he obliterates himself, the revelations of the new world flow into him. Only a high grade of such selfless surrender enables a man to receive the higher spiritual facts that surround him on all sides.

We can consciously develop this capacity in ourselves. We can try, for example, to refrain from any judgment on people around us. We should obliterate within ourselves the gauge of "attractive" and "repellent," of "stupid" or "clever," that we are accustomed to apply, and try without this gauge to understand persons purely from and through themselves. The best exercises can be made with people for whom one has an aversion. We should suppress this aversion with all our power and allow everything that they do to affect us without bias. . . . This openminded and uncritical laying of ourselves open has nothing whatever to do with blind faith. The important thing is not that we should believe blindly in anything, *but that we should not put a blind judgment in the place of the living impression* (italics mine) (Steiner, 1971).

In the larger context of Rudolf Steiner's writings, it is clear that by the word "suppression" of an aversion or a judgment, he does not refer to the elimination of some specific impulse by a will-power exercised by one part of the person to control another part. He says repeatedly that what must come first is the taking of a central attitude for which he uses such words as "make of himself an empty vessel" or "complete inner selflessness" or "selfless surrender" or "be able . . . to obliterate himself with all his prejudices." These phrases as used by Rudolf Steiner refer to what we are calling the transformational process. They describe the centered Self that can allow things and people to tell us about themselves as they are, apart from what we may project upon them.

Freedom from prejudiced, personally-generated judgment does not remove from us the ability to "receive the living impression" and to be affected by it—but without bias. The ability to discern the meaning of what is really present is sharpened, not destroyed. One has a new capacity to perceive the truth of a situation, in its wholeness, and thus to be able to respond appropriately to it and to make sound decisions concerning it. This is a discernment or a discrimination rather than a conditioned value judgment.

The integrated Self approaches each thing, person, event, with a willingness to see it as it is. Rather than immediately having an emotional *re*-action based on conditioned judgments, the centered Self looks at what is there, accepts in the moment that that is how it is, makes a discernment about what it is and then acts (not *re*-acts) with an appropriate response. Rather than to "have one's buttons pushed" in an automatic, conditioned *re*-action, one allows an accurate assessment of the situation to emerge from what is really going on.

The centered Self does not come to the situation with a pre-judgment of how the thing "ought" to be. It can allow an instant of recognition that the situation is what it is, before acting in relation to it. This may be an instantaneous inner happening, but it represents a crucial element in the person's ability to respond appropriately to what is really going on.

It is the prior commitment to Willingness . . . WHATEVER which permits the clear perception and allows us to see what all the circumstances call for from us as a response. Here we have an answer to the question, "But how will I know what represents wholeness?" Fortunately for us, the knowledge of what life is wanting us to do is remarkably available to us when we are not making value judgments but are wanting only to respond appropriately and inclusively to what is really going on. The whole area of intuitive knowing is then wide open to us.

We discover that the hard, significant question is not, "What is appropriate in this situation, viewed inclusively?" The essential question which must be answered first is, *"Would I be willing to do it, WHATEVER it might be?"* With that question wholeheartedly answered in advance, in the state of centered willingness, the undreamed-of vastness of our consciousness can provide us with the answers we need for our personal decisions and the broader decisions affecting our world.

One of the most significant results of this coming to each situation without preconditioned value judgments is the vast improvement in the appropriateness and therefore in the effectiveness of the response which is made. This ability to act from centered willingness to do WHATEVER represents wholeness can revolutionize decision making because the appropriateness of an action is viewed from the widest, most inclusive perspective possible. Large institutions, corporate and governmental, have begun to explore how their decision-makers can be better able to respond without narrow, conditioned pre-judgments (Harman, 1978).

Two men of my acquaintance who are pioneering in such work with business and government are Dr. Arthur Hastings and Dr. Willis W. Harman. Arthur Hastings, past-president of the Association for Transpersonal Psychology, serves as a consultant to groups wishing to improve the soundness and effectiveness of their decision-making and decisionmakers. It is out of the breadth of his own awareness of the transformational process that Arthur can approach the specific problems of an organization.

Willis Harman, professor of Engineering-Economic Systems at Stanford University and Associate Director, Center for the Study of Social Policy, SRI International, is in the forefront of an effort to relate new methods of decisionmaking to societal futures for the planet. The first time that I read an article by Bill Harman in the *Journal of the Association for Transpersonal Psychology* several years ago I thought, "He's so clear. I wonder how he got so clear." Later when I read the excellent interview with him in *New Realities* magazine (Bolen, 1978), at the time that he became president of the Institute of Noetic Sciences, I found out how he got so clear. The editor, James Bolen, was asking Bill about his own transformational journey. Bill replied that it had begun for him fifteen years before at a Sequoia Seminar.

As I read the words, all the lights flashed on and all the bells began to ring and I knew why I sensed such clarity in Bill's writings. He too had had an opportunity to be touched, indirectly, by the brilliant, razor-sharp, incisively questioning mind of Dr. Henry Burton Sharman and his *Records of the Life of Jesus.* The Sequoia Seminar, in the Santa Cruz mountains of California, is led by Harry and Emelia Rathbun who were in the first faculty group I led at Stanford in 1931! Harry was then a law professor, and in the years since, following study with Dr. Sharman, he and Emelia founded and developed a group called Creative Initiative Foundation, centered in Palo Alto. An indication of their views and of their work is given in Harry's book, *Creative Initiative: Guide to Fulfillment* (Rathbun, 1976).

Of course I made a contact with Willis Harman and with his wife, Charlene. Now there is with both of them this fine sense of deep connection and of having known them always. Bill's rigorous scientific training is a perfect background for his interest in consciousnesss and in intuitive knowing. At present he is using it concretely to show how group decisionmaking can be affected by the openness of the centered willingness state.

After recounting, simply and clearly, some extremely cogent experimental evidence of the unsuspected available knowledge and powers of our minds, Willis Harman wrote in the Institute of Noetic Sciences Newsletter (1978):

> Most of us are quite aware of the workings of some mysterious creative process which works outside of our conscious awareness but quietly remains available to help with our really tough problems. Business executives, scientists, inventors, poets and composers, all have repeatedly told us of the creative experience. Having exhausted every apparent lead to solution of a difficult problem, one turns it over to this behind-the-scenes creative center which in due course, perhaps awakening one in the middle of the night, presents the key to the solution. Sometimes this answer is in easily recognizable form; sometimes in veiled imagery. But one marvels at the beauty and appropriateness of the solution which had previously seemed to be inaccessible.
>
> Now there is a next logical step beyond that recognition of the creative process, which relatively few people seem to take. If that creative unconscious part of myself is so much more knowledgeable and wise than my conscious mind, why stop at submitting to it only specific and difficult problems? *Why not turn over the whole of one's life?* (Italics mine).

(Perhaps you can see why, when I first read those words, I danced a jig and felt the wonderful sense of oneness that one experiences with someone who understands and clearly enunciates, out of his own particular life-experience, the essence of the transformational process).

Bill Harman went on to write:

One notices, of course, that that is precisely what is recommended in the "perennial wisdom" of the various religious traditions of the world. And now we see a still greater significance to the findings regarding remote viewing, psychokinesis, and the rest of the psychic phenomena. If all have these potentialities and understand them, albeit unconsciously, then the arguments by which a generation of scientists arrogantly proclaimed the spiritual nature of man to be disproven—those arguments were not valid. Claims of faith healing and the efficacy of prayer, and assorted kinds of miracles are not *a priori* superstitious nonsense. If minds are truly joined, so that a flashing light in one person's eyes is detected in the mind of a second, remotely located person, then there is more to the religious concept of love than physical attraction or reasoned altruism. . . .

If (a) I have access to a creative goalsetting and problem-solving capacity of unlimited potentiality, (b) minds are joined, and (c) ultimately mind and spirit are dominant over the physical, then this suggests something revolutionary with regard to group decisionmaking. When minds join in asking for direction and assistance, by their very affirmation they tend to bring that guidance and help into existence. And if a group of individuals are responsible for decisions that affect the future welfare of an entire society, then it is especially important that they not settle for less than the superior guidance which is obtainable in this way. That is the highest form of leadership.

CHAPTER 16

Acceptance of Others
and of Ourselves

L ETTING GO OF value judgments is closely related to acceptance. In a non-emotional, unbiased acceptance,
the ability to see what to do is enhanced by the open state
of willingness . . . WHATEVER.

An important point needs to be clarified here. The acceptance which I am describing is not acceptance in the sense
of passive agreement to allow what is happening to continue to happen. The *action* which the integrated Self comes
to see as appropriate in a specific circumstance may be no
action at all or it may require action to reverse the situation
completely. But before any decision is made or any action
is taken, there is this wholehearted recognition and acceptance that the situation is whatever it is.

In ordinary states of consciousness which do not issue
from a centered, unified Self but rather from one or
another of our sub-personalities, our relationships are com-

plicated by the fact that we do not accept others as they are. Instead, we are wanting them to be different and we make endless efforts, subtle or gross, to change them.

Take the example of my husband and me throughout our marriage. We never ceased to want the other to be different. We did not accept one another as we were; we were constantly putting expectations on the other partner. We were not accepting parts of ourselves and were projecting those unowned parts out onto the other person, and then rejecting what we saw in them "out there." One instance of that is that I had difficulty in recognizing and fully embracing my own dependency needs. I projected them on Bert, making him more of an invalid than he needed to be. Then I inwardly and unawarely berated him for not being the big strong man I needed to lean on to meet my own dependency needs.

The issue of acceptance brings us face to face with what the transformational process calls for from us if we are to find fulfillment. While we are centering ourselves by an inner attitude of wanting one thing, we cannot be wanting someone else to change. That would be a violation of the process we are engaged in for our own well-being.

We are helped out of such an attitude as we come to learn from more and more experience that nothing that anyone else can do or not do can feed our deepest hunger or make a "wrong" situation "right." We are nourished by our connection with our Source, the wholeness. In that connected state we can accept others as they are, thus giving them the freedom to move, if they wish to, toward their maximum potential.

Because my own training has been in psychology and psychotherapy, I am aware of different degrees of acceptance which can be given by a therapist depending upon whether or not he or she is actively involved with this transformational process. A cardinal feature of the training of any psychotherapist is "Know thyself," and another is "Accept your client where he or she is."

Conscientious therapists attempt to do both, but the results for the person who comes for help are inevitably limited by the level of personal integration of the therapist. The ultimate choice of how to use the help belongs to the client, but the client's ability to move and to resolve the problems will be immeasurably enhanced if the acceptance of the client by the therapist flows from a generalized, centered willingness to express WHATEVER represents wholeness.

This kind of acceptance, deep and genuine, does not mean agreement with what the person does, or is, or feels. It is acceptance of the person's right to choose what he does or is or feels and to take the consequences of those choices. This level of acceptance allows the therapist to see the client as he is and not as the therapist wishes he were. The acceptance has a remarkably freeing effect on what the therapist perceives, and may have an amazing effect upon actions and attitudes of the client.

An enrichment of my appreciation of the meaning of acceptance came to me in the work I did with a woman who was facing the possibility of cancer (Chapter 19). The issue soon became, for her, "Do I really want to live, or is it possible that I want to die?" I had to plumb new depths in myself as to the meaning of acceptance in order to be able to give her total freedom to explore both possibilities without any pressure from me in either direction.

In a therapeutic relationship, acceptance means, in the most profound sense, relating to the essential core of the person; it means seeing him or her as a whole being, on the journey toward full maturity. In a case of life and death, acceptance means trusting WHATEVER it is within the person that allows the making of that choice, in line with the individual's own inner growth, WHATEVER form that may take.

Self-acceptance is much harder than acceptance of someone else. I guess what I mean by that is that with certain kinds of training and techniques, a degree of acceptance of others may be achieved, but *self*-acceptance demands that one *be* the integrated Self. The sense of separation and lack which are characteristic of the usual self must be replaced by the sense of oneness and nourishment which come from being centered in willingness . . . WHATEVER, if one is to escape the torments of non-acceptance of oneself.

Very early in life we begin to form the sense of being separate and isolated from things and from people. We experiment with all sorts of ways to get what we want from what we feel to be an alien environment. We look to others for nourishment, acceptance, approbation, love, and evidence of our worth, and we pay any price required. You have seen some of the prices I have paid. The measure of our worth becomes what others think of us. This is a fatal trap from which various schools of psychology attempt to extricate us.

But the question remains, "If I see that it is hopeless to look to others for my own validation, how do I validate myself? How do I come to accept my own worth?" The validation comes from my identification with What Is, with wholeness, WHATEVER that may be.

We can never find self-validation while we continue to compare ourselves with others. To do that is to place emotional value judgments upon ourselves. It can undermine our courage, cause us to doubt the efficacy of this whole process, paralyze our effectiveness, make us label ourselves hopeless failures, and cause untold misery. Comparisons go when the centered Self is in place.

There is then really only the one question to ask. "Am I totally willing to do, feel, be WHATEVER is wanting to express as my whole Self?" The only point of reference is my own center, my source. Am I there? Is all of me collected, ready, integrated, open to allow WHATEVER wants to express as me, in each moment? If so, I am meeting the condition for my own wholeness, and I am contributing my part to the wholeness I seek to serve in fulfilling my highest potential. I identify myself as wholeness being me.

There is one yardstick. I measure myself against that and against nothing else and no one else. As I do this, and begin to see my wholeness expressing the wholeness, I open to the possibility that I may be more than I thought I was. If I am not separate after all, but am an integral part of the whole, I have some purpose or meaning in relation to that. If the whole is expressing variously in all the parts, my form of its expression has as much validity as anyone else's, as long as I am opening to allow the flow of WHATEVER. My sole concern is to open and allow the expression of wholeness as me, no matter what I am doing.

This is the difference between *Doing* and *Being*. While I am not accepting myself, I have nowhere to look except at my Doing, in order to measure my acceptability. And it is by my Doing that others measure my acceptability, in accordance with their own particular value judgments and projections.

However, when I can accept myself as wholeness being me, I am in one state of Being, out of which all of my Doing will result naturally and inevitably. I take care to BE at my center, in this willingness state, and what I DO will "follow as the night the day."

This is freedom. This is how I drop forever the bag of stones I have been carrying on my back, through lack of self-acceptance. I can let it all go. I begin to sense the oneness of which I am a part. I am life being itself as me. Life asks no more of me and I ask no more of myself.

From what you know of my life story, you can see that self-acceptance is for me a deeply important hurdle. The freedom which it brings is worth all of the pain it takes to teach me this elementary lesson.

CHAPTER 17

Forgiveness

THE FOUR AREAS we are looking at—freedom from value judgments; acceptance of others and of oneself; forgiveness; and love . . . WHATEVER, have this in common; they are all fruits of wanting the one thing. They flow naturally and spontaneously from an integrated center. My own experience has been that they are all possible because a sense of separateness gradually passes, replaced by a realization of oneness. We begin to experience the connection between all that we are, and all that is; between the personal will and "what wants to happen"; between wholeness and all of its parts; between us and nature, whether it is blossoming or rotting, living or dying; between us and all other people, "good" or "bad."

With that realization, the moment comes when we discover that there is no "other." We begin to find out that, despite all apparent evidence to the contrary, we are all one in a wholeness, and whatever we see in anyone else, "good" or "bad," is a mirror of something which exists in our consciousness, or we could not be seeing it in the "outer." This helps us to deal with the projections we unconsciously put onto others, projections which are destructive to ourselves and which prevent real, honest, enriching relationships with others. This realization allows us to begin to see that there is nothing in "your" consciousness which is not in "my" consciousness. "Consciousness," WHATEVER that may be, includes it all.

True forgiveness, freeing to the one who forgives and to the one who is forgiven, occurs naturally and without effort to the integrated Self which begins to experience connectedness, oneness. Why does this happen?

My experience is that forgiveness comes about as we are able to recognize in ourselves, in the "offender," and in all mankind, similar human qualities which are inherent in specific attachments. We may possess these attributes in varying degrees and in different areas, but the potentials are in us all. To admit to ourselves that our wholeness includes the potential for all kinds of emotion and all kinds of action is not easy, but that recognition, at a deep level, permits a compassion which is impossible otherwise.

Instead of condemning and damning the specific acts of others, we can see these acts as the inevitable, not really surprising outcomes of a particular level of awareness with which we are fully familiar. We are foolish if we expect other people's "sins" (or our own) to change without the profound inner shift from wanting many things to wanting only one thing. The outer expressions are not going to change significantly without the inner change to the integrated willingness state.

And there is an even deeper aspect to forgiveness. The

need for me to forgive anyone for anything occurs only because I believe that someone has harmed me, has "done me wrong." But such a description is meaningless to the centered Self. No one has the power to harm me or to do me wrong. My well-being or lack of it results solely from my own inner attitude. At any given moment, I am centered in willingness . . . WHATEVER, or I am not. This alone determines my essential well-being, no matter what may be happening, even to the extremity of physical death, at the hands of whomever or whatever. This inner attitude is the true Source of my life.

Thus, no matter what someone has done, I have no need to forgive him for wronging me, because he has not "wronged me." He does not possess that power over the integrated Self. If he has not acted from his center, he will get the results which come from that. If he has acted from his center (whether or not I recognize it), he will get the results which come from that. In both cases, each of us is dealing inwardly with life as a whole, and the only meaningful transaction is between each self and the whole.

While we are not too far from the idea of self-acceptance which I was presenting in the last chapter, it is well to remember to forgive ourselves when we fail to forgive others for an apparent wrong. We do the best we can; if we are not centered, we'll do things that we regret and we may then flagellate ourselves for having done them. We may even beat ourselves for not forgiving someone who, we are sure, had our best interests at heart, but who still "hurt" us deeply. We need to laugh at ourselves for such foolishness, not beat ourselves. We need only to center once more. From that perspective we see that of course there are parts of us that will do and feel and say foolish, senseless things. But the way out is not to stir up a lot of dust with self-recriminations. The way out is quietly to center once again and to invite wholeness to use all that we are, appropriately.

To extend the meaning of forgiveness a bit further, we are apt to jump to the question, "But what if my condemnation and resentment at the actions of the 'offender' result not from what he has 'done to me' but rather from what he has done to innocent, helpless victims?"

The principle is the same. In both instances, if we are centered in willingness—committed to express WHATEVER the whole situation requires of us—NO ONE CAN SAY what we will *do* in the specific circumstance, whether it involves us or others. All that we know is that it will be the most appropriate thing we can see to do under the optimum condition for seeing anything: namely, willingness to do WHATEVER our most expanded awareness of the situation shows to us.

But the action we may be led to take in a particular situation involving ourselves or others is a totally different thing from the issue of whether we feel condemnation or whether we feel forgiveness in relation to the "evil-doer." Some of the most moving moments in history are those describing an outpouring of forgiveness by a "victim" towards an "offender." The implication which emerges from these transcendent examples is that the whole concept of forgiveness is without meaning, since the one who forgives is relating to and not condemning the essence of the aggressor, and is therefore feeling no separation from but only a oneness with the essence or divinity or wholeness of the aggressor. This oneness is affirmed in the "forgiveness."

It is when we thus feel ourselves to be part of an all-inclusive wholeness, of which everyone and everything is also a part, that we realize that our fulfillment and well-being lie only in this feeling of being connected with our Source, and separate from nothing and from no one. Then we know that the only "harm" that can come to us is to feel separated from the Source, the wholeness. For this reason, in the ultimate sense, no one can "harm" another person and therefore no "forgiveness" is necessary.

I am realizing that two rather recent influences in my life have enriched my understanding of this. One is the contact I have had with Tibetan Buddhism, primarily with Nyingma Institute in Berkeley, founded by Tarthang Tulku. The concept of the oneness of all is clearly apparent. Another writer on Buddhism who speaks from an all-embracing perspective of this kind is Lama Govinda, whose *Creative Meditation and Multi-Dimensional Consciousness* is a luminous work. Also I am impressed by the clarity of George Marshall's biography, *Buddha: The Quest for Serenity,* which is enriched by an excellent introduction by Huston Smith.

The other recent influence in my life, out of a different tradition, is *A Course in Miracles.* This is a three-volume work, put together by an anonymous woman psychologist, born a Jew but without a religious faith of her own, who found herself channeling material purporting to be from Jesus. Although the terminology is different from that which I am using, I have found that the core teaching clearly indicates a level of personal integration possible only to a centered Self. One of the basic tenets concerns forgiveness, which is seen to be the inevitable result of the experience of oneness, of wholeness. One of the volumes of *A Course in Miracles* is a workbook of three hundred and sixty-five lessons, arranged progressively to aid a student in moving step by step to the new perspective. I am impressed by the caliber of the growing number of persons who are using this particular scaffolding as a means to wanting one thing.

We are, and we always have been, and we always will be an integral part of a totality. Nothing and no one can change that. What can change is our belief in the separation, and our belief in the necessity to continue the sense of separation. It is this which creates all the experiences which follow from the belief that we are separate from our Source: isolation, vulnerability, fear, guilt and the need to attack and to defend.

It is by our living through and recognizing the hopelessness of continuing on this level of awareness that we have the possibility of seeing, at last, that no one has the power to harm us. This liberates us from feeling the victim of anyone or anything "outside" of us. We can then drop the fear; we have no need to attack and no need to defend. In our defenselessness we are invulnerable, because we are part of the oneness, and there is no enemy to defend against.

It is then, at a very deep level, and from our single, generalized intention, that we experience the fact that the only thing that can "harm" us is our own choice to be closed to "WHATEVER is wanting to express through us." It is this refusal alone which is to us "worse than death."

In my own life I recall that from the time I was in my teens I was deeply touched by the passages in Plato which describe the trial and death of Socrates. Here was a man in the fifth century B.C. who seems to us to have been honestly doing everything in his power to teach the truth as he saw it. The result was that he was accused of corrupting the youth of Athens, and was put on trial for his life. During the proceedings, Socrates was offered two alternatives to the sentence of death by poison. He could have saved his life by ceasing to teach or by going into exile. His friends pleaded with him to accept one of these alternatives, but he chose death instead.

Why? Because, as he explained to his grieving friends, that which gave meaning and fulfillment to his life was to obey the still small voice which he heard within him, guiding his actions day by day. To him, his voluntarily chosen obedience to this inner direction was indeed the Source of his life. To save his physical life by going against the clear counsel of his inner voice, would to him have been, literally, a fate worse than death. His choice to drink the poison represented neither a denial nor a loss nor a sacrifice but rather the fulfillment of his deepest desire which was to remain attuned and obedient to his inner commitment to what he called The Good. This total commitment made him, in the most profound sense, invulnerable to anything harmful, including physical death.

Twenty-five hundred years later, I am inspired by Plato's accounts of the quiet, cheerful conversations in the prison between Socrates and his friends, in which he is sustained by his conviction that "no evil can happen to a good man, either in life or after death." When Crito begs him to allow his friends to arrange for his escape, Socrates explains that his inner guidance forbids this. "This is the voice which I seem to hear murmuring in my ears, like the sound of the flute in the ears of the mystic; that voice, I say, is humming in my ears and prevents me from hearing any other. And I know that anything more which you will say will be in vain. Yet speak, if you have anything to say.

Crito: I have nothing to say, Socrates.

Socrates: Then let me follow the intimations of the will of God" (Eliot, Ed., 1937).

The extremity of a choice such as that of Socrates shocks us and makes us want to close our minds and run away. But it can equally illuminate for us the essential meaning of the transformational process as I am defining it. Socrates did not "want to die," nor did he "want to live." In the place of these wants and all other specific desires, he had substituted a single, abstract want, i.e., to follow the appropriate direction indicated to him by an inner prompting. It was in his voluntary obedience to that inner voice that he fulfilled his Self. True Self-realization and Self-fulfillment resulted for him from following these inner dictates.

It is for this reason that I have alleged that "his choice to drink the poison represented neither a denial nor a loss nor a sacrifice but rather the fulfillment of his deepest desire." His deepest desire was not to die. His deepest desire was to maintain the connection between himself and his Source, which was represented for him by the inner direction he received for his life and his daily actions. He was doing what he wanted to do.

But how about the rest of us ordinary mortals who are not aware of a clear voice which recommends for or against a particular action? This question is vitally important and it is the same question as, "How do I know what represents wholeness?"

The answer from my own life and the lives of others I have touched is that the knowledge of what to do comes out of the state of non-attachment. First must come the undefined single intention—"I want only to allow the expression of WHATEVER is the most appropriate, inclusive response, moment by moment." This is the willingness state with the openness and readiness to consider any and all options, unconditionally. There is a toti-potential in each moment.

Out of this non-attached and non-resisting state emerges an indication of what "wants to happen." I scarcely dare to theorize on how this can be so. Yet it is not too difficult to speculate on what may occur, as we now begin to see that the most modern sub-atomic physics, the most modern transpersonal psychology, and the most modern and most ancient mysticism all strongly suggest an essential unity in the universe. What I call "my consciousness," when it is not holding onto nor resisting specifics, is opening to a vaster, more inclusive consciousness which excludes no one and no thing.

In this willingness state, open to wholeness . . . WHATEVER, the intuition with which I am endowed is able to function fully and freely. The direction which I receive for my actions is then consistent with an inclusive, unconditionally loving view which sees the oneness in all things.

This provides what is actually another mode of knowledge. Its way of working is revealed in what Satprem writes about the experience of Sri Aurobindo (Satprem, 1968), who describes as follows, this growing ability to contact "the vibration of silence" in a place deep within.

Gradually, in fact, we find that it is not necessary to think, that something behind or above does the work, with a precision and an infallibility growing ever greater as we get into the habit of referring to it; that it is not necessary to remember but at the required moment the exact indication comes up, not necessary to plan one's action but a secret spring sets it going without one's willing it or thinking about it and makes us do exactly what is needed with a wisdom and a foresight of which our mind, always short-sighted, is quite incapable. And we see that the more we obey these swift intimations, these lightning suggestions, the more they become frequent, clear, imperious, habitual, somewhat like an intuitive process but with this important difference that our intuitions are almost always blurred by the mind which, moreover, excels in imitating them and in making us take its whims for revelations, whilst here the transmission is clear, exact, for the good reason that the mind is dumb. But we all have the experience of those problems "mysteriously" solved in sleep, that is, precisely when the thinking machine is hushed. No doubt there will be errors and blunders before the new working is established with any surety, but the seeker must be ready to make mistakes in order to learn; in fact, he will find that the mistake comes always from an intrusion of the mind; each time the mind intervenes, it blurs everything, splits up everything, impedes everything. . . .

The mind jams everything, because it desires, because it fears, because it wants, and nothing reaches it which is not immediately falsified by this desire, this fear, this will. . . . With the silent mind comes a widening of the consciousness and it can turn at will towards any point of the universal reality to know there what it needs to know.

CHAPTER 18

Love . . . WHATEVER

W E HAVE LOOKED at the releasing of value judgments, and at acceptance, and forgiveness, as manifestations of the centered inner attitude of wanting only to express the wholeness which we are. In my view, these results cannot really be experienced without the foundation of the single intention, from which they flow naturally.

Implicit in all of them, and in a sense including all of them, is another manifestation of the centered willingness state. That is an expansive, unconditional love which is truly a love . . . WHATEVER. To me, none of the wonders of the integrated, centered life is more deeply moving than the power of this feeling-state which emanates from the centered Self, from wholeness. This level of expression, to which we may give the name of unconditional love, has nothing whatever in common with the usual level of human "love." Rather, it is an accepting recognition of the other person's essential beingness, and thus a trust in his right and his ability to make his own choices and to pursue his own soul's growth. This level of unconditional, non-emotional, non-judgmental love transforms our personal relationships and it could transform our planet, if enough of us tried it.

Experience shows that as we individually center in the silent inner place of willingness and commitment, we are led to act spontaneously towards others with an unconditional love. We may even be surprised to find ourselves increasingly able to give this unpossessive, non-demanding, non-judgmental love to a wider and wider spectrum of people, things, and events. As we function out of the centered willingness . . . WHATEVER state, an expansiveness occurs, an inclusiveness, without even a target to receive it. It just is; it radiates and it expresses its beingness as limitless love . . . WHATEVER. Its effect is transforming, wherever it goes.

That kind of love is possible only to someone who feels deeply within himself that WHATEVER the universe is, it is a whole; it is one system; and whatever is happening to one part of it is affecting it all. Whether we like it or not, we are all one. Thus, unconditional love is the quality that expresses wholeness.

In Lawrence LeShan's excellent book, *The Medium, the Mystic, and the Physicist,* he gives a passage from Albert Einstein which to me adds richness to this concept.

> A human being is a part of the whole, called by us the "Universe," a part limited in time and space. He experiences himself, his thoughts and feelings as something separated from the rest—a kind of optical delusion of his consciousness. This delusion is a kind of prison for us, restricting us to our personal desires and to affection for a few persons nearest to us. Our task must be to free ourselves from this prison by widening our circle of compassion to embrace all living creatures and the whole of nature

in its beauty. Nobody is able to achieve this completely, but the striving for such achievement is in itself a part of the liberation and a foundation for inner security (LeShan, 1966).

In the transformational process, we are surrendered to WHATEVER seems appropriate in the moment, viewed as inclusively as our expanding awareness permits. Then we begin to find out that often the WHATEVER turns out to be that we act towards others with unconditional love. Who knows what WHATEVER is, in any universal sense? And yet the evidence is all around us that WHATEVER is wanting to express in human life includes such opposites as life and death, growth and decay, construction and destruction, chaos and harmony, which we may come to see as one unending process of which we are a part. And our part appears to be to learn to love it all, limitlessly.

Throughout my life I have had many opportunities to "love" and I have done so "after my fashion" with as much or as little awareness as was available to me at the time. Out of all the experiences, I can report one conclusion about loving, and it is this: an unconditional love, without jealousy or possessiveness or demands or expectations, is impossible except from an integrated Self, centered in wanting only to express wholeness.

This single inner attitude is the essential prerequisite for the ability to give unconditional love. Such a love flows only from a sense of universal oneness, which is an identification with the whole. Despite all appearances to the contrary, unconditional love can see each person or situation as representing an aspect of the whole. Such love is both a natural, and at the same time a seemingly miraculous expression of the being who emerges through the transformational process. Without the basic single intention, a love . . . WHATEVER is impossible.

From all of this it is apparent that the usual spectrum of human love is to be found at a completely different level from what I am calling love . . . WHATEVER, or limitless love, or unconditional love. Almost all of the human love which we see or experience is coming from an uncentered self, a self which wants and therefore is attached to many things and people and circumstances.

When we honestly examine the "love" given by the uncentered self, we can find the unseen strings which are attached to it. The uncentered self says, "I love you" but it is also saying, "Of course I want you to love me in return." It says, "I love you but of course it is only fair that you should understand me, and meet my emotional needs even without my voicing those needs."

The uncentered self is accurately described in popular love songs. For example: You belong to me. . . . I am yours, body and soul. . . . Some day I'll know that moment divine when all the things you are are mine. . . . I am yours and you are mine forever. . . . O, promise me that. . . .

From the new perspective of the centered Self, we come to see that the giving or receiving of specific promises is a denial of the central attitude of willingness . . . WHATEVER, in which the commitment of each person is to an undefined, inclusive wholeness, and never to a pre-determined, limited condition. The essence of love from the center is unconditional, without limits.

An uncentered self may wail in "righteous" anguish, "How can you not love me after all that I have done for you?" The strings which were attached to that love as it was given out, however lavishly and "unselfishly," are apparent to us when we view it from a heightened perspective.

"I need your love. Only you can satisfy my longing. You are my life." The person to whom these words are said may glow with the warmth of being needed, of being exclusively chosen, of being found indispensable to someone else's happiness. But all of this is based on a fallacy. The truth is that, in the deepest sense, no one has the power to make another person happy and no one has the power to make another person unhappy. That power resides only within the individual person who relates the self to the whole. To ask that another person provide this for us is to court disaster, sooner or later.

In our culture, conditional love is so ever-present that we can scarcely open our minds to the possibility of something in human relationships which is so different that it appears to come from another dimension. And it does. It comes from a level of consciousness in which we can see and love people as they are, asking nothing in return. It's a love which flows from our fullness, not from our need. We do not need to seek fulfillment from the other person because our fulfillment comes from our connection with the Source, of which we are a part. We do not belong to anyone nor does anyone belong to us. Our lives belong to life itself, to the wholeness of What Is. The unconditional love we experience is an expression of the appreciation we feel for life in WHATEVER form we find it. We begin to love and appreciate wholeness by seeing it in others and in ourselves.

To end this segment on unconditional love, I'd like to look back once again at the thirty years of my relationship with my husband, Bert Horn. An obvious question to ask is, "If you had been functioning as a centered Self all of that time, what would you have been doing? What would have been different?"

My first answer has to be, "I don't know." If I had been embracing all the parts of myself, my own wholeness, I might never have responded to Bert as a person to share my life and to receive the projections of the unowned parts of myself. If I had wanted one thing only, I would not have *wanted* Bert's love, nor would I have *needed* it. In the centered state, I might or might not have joined my life with his in a partnership or marriage. I do not know. But WHATEVER the specifics of my life, the deepest springs and true Source of my nourishment, joy, fulfillment, would have been my openness to express the wholeness with which I identified myself.

If I had been centered and had thus loved Bert unconditionally, I could not have been torn apart as I was by the Tanya episodes and his wish to have an open marriage. My deep satisfaction would have proceeded from my own sense of connection with my Source, the oneness, the centered willingness state, and not from anything Bert was doing or not doing.

What would I have said when Bert suggested an exploration of the sexual element in the "second circle" of Kunkel's diagram about relationships? I do not know. There are various possibilities: I believe that I could have agreed wholeheartedly and without conflict, *if* the idea seemed appropriate from my centered state. Or, I could have agreed to it for him but not for me, or for me but not for him. Or, I could have said "No" and my relationship with Bert might have gone on, or I could have said "No" and broken the relationship.

But whatever might have happened in the external circumstances would not have been the important issue *if* my predominant state had been that of wanting one thing. Had that been true, no matter what the circumstances, *I would have had what I wanted,* because what I wanted would have been to be open to allow WHATEVER represented wholeness, viewed as inclusively as I could see it. This would have freed me from attachment or resistance to any of the possible options.

As I have been writing these last chapters, I have been increasingly aware of how strange and even inhuman some of my observations must seem. The transformational process itself represents a monumental change in the organization of the human psyche. To want only something generalized, undefined, in advance of a specific situation, is strange enough. But the kind of implications I have been suggesting may seem even more bizarre: the freedom from pre-conditioned value judgments; the possibility of profound, non-egotistical self-acceptance and acceptance of other people and events; "forgiveness" so deep that it comes from a feeling that no "sin" has been committed and therefore no "forgiveness" is needed; an unconditional love which contains no possessiveness, jealousy, or attachment yet illuminates the lives of those who feel it and express it inclusively, and which may transform those it touches. These are not commonplace attitudes.

Perhaps it is enough if I convey to you my own deep sense that the transformational process in the human individual is not simply one more modification of behavior by some technique or other. Rather, it is a complete shift in the object of our will and the organization of the whole Self. That substitution of one want for all the other wants is the essence of the change in consciousness. It is simple but it is very difficult to establish and to maintain, granted the eons of time during which specific desires have been humanity's way of coping with the environment.

Because it is so difficult and at times seems so alien, it is essential that we see why anyone would start it or continue it. The answer is abundantly clear: It works. This transformational process provides for the individual a stable sense of well-being, of desire fulfilled, of self-realization, freedom, a deep joy, an equanimity amidst turmoil, and an ever-expanding ability to love. It would provide for human society the basis for solving all the problems which we face as planetary citizens. For these reasons it seems to me worth whatever effort it requires from me to learn to live it and to convey its essence as clearly as I possibly can.

CHAPTER 19

Toward Transformation
Through Cancer

IN THIS EFFORT to describe the transformtional process from a psychological viewpoint, I am going to give you an example of an individual life in which I have been privileged to watch that process taking place.

It all began in my "second half of life" period when I was exploring parapsychology, holograms, and a holistic approach to health and illness in which the emphasis is not primarily on the disease but rather on the whole person who is having the disease.

Friends in Carmel told me about a place in southern California called Meadowlark, in Hemet, a pioneer example of an unusual residential treatment center based upon this "holistic" view of health. My interest was caught, not because I was especially in need of treatment, but because I learned that the founder and medical director, Dr. Evarts G. Loomis, had recently taken a group to Europe to visit a number of his friends and fellow-physicians and surgeons who were deeply involved in "Medicine for the Whole Person."

As it happened, I was planning to spend several months in Europe and so I decided to "sample" Meadowlark, and to learn from Dr. Loomis and others who had been with him, whether I might perhaps experience some of the same people and centers that had enriched their journey the previous year.

Meadowlark turned out to be a remarkable place with a devoted staff which, under Dr. Loomis' leadership was indeed, in a very creative way, treating the whole person—body, mind, and spirit—rather than the disease. The philosophy is well expressed in a book which Dr. Loomis co-authored with J. Sig Paulson, *Healing for Everyone: Medicine of the Whole Person* (Loomis and Paulson, 1979).

This first visit led to my meeting a number of like-minded physicians in Europe, among them Dr. Paul Tournier of Geneva who has become a valued friend. I know of no one who sees more clearly than he the essence of the transformational process. He believes from his years of practice that no permanent solution to disease, physical or mental, is possible without that inner transformation (Tournier 1957, 1965, 1972).

On one of my subsequent visits to Meadowlark I met and had a conversation with Mrs. Gertrude Karnow, a member of the staff who had recently come from the Los Angeles area, where for many years she had had her own practice as a psychotherapist. Dr. Loomis, other staff members, and guests expressed to me their appreciation of her presence at Meadowlark and her skill as a counselor.

About five months later, when I had returned from several months in Europe, I was surprised to receive a telephone call from Mrs. Karnow. She had heard that I might be coming to Meadowlark and she wondered if she might talk with me. A couple of months before, she had discovered a lump in her right breast. She had consulted two physicians who were her friends, Dr. Evarts Loomis and Dr. Brugh Joy, both of whom had strongly urged that she have a biopsy, and if a malignancy were found, that she proceed with necessary surgery.

She told me that she had not been able to do this. Something very strong in her was "refusing to have her body mutilated." She had a well-developed sense of the spiritual within herself and she believed it could be an ally as she faced this problem. In addition, she was accepting the importance of nutrition and had placed herself on a diet consisting mainly of raw fruits and vegetables.

However, time was passing and the lump was still present. She knew that I had begun to do a little work with persons facing cancer and she asked to see me, if I were coming soon to Meadowlark. I told her that my plans had changed and that I would not be going to southern California for several weeks. She then asked if she could come up to Carmel to talk with me.

This was a crucial moment for both of us. As I learned later, her asking for help, and from an almost complete stranger, was totally unlike her life-long pattern of *giving,* and not asking for things for herself. This telephone call, she said later, came from a kind of desperation, "from a very deep place in me that *knew.* It's like a voice that says, 'This is what you do.' It's a good example of the fact that the intuitive knowledge is there."

For my part, her request presented obstacles. She was telling me that she was absolutely, adamantly refusing to have her body cut into, even for a biopsy. This sounded foolhardy in the extreme, and probably deadly. Also, my personal plans made it inconvenient to go south just then, and I knew, too, that the circumstances in Carmel would not be conducive to our working together then. On an impulse, I asked whether she and her husband would have room for me in their home if I were to go down. She said yes.

In that moment, something very deep in me said, "Go."

It was irrational in view of all the "sensible" considerations, but it was unmistakably clear. And in that same moment I knew that the only possible way I could be of help to her would be to accept totally the fact that she was refusing any form of surgical intervention. I would go to stay with her and we would begin where she was.

Apart from my basic training and experience as a therapist, there were three major facets to my preparation for the work I was doing with cancer. The first was what I had learned from Dr. O. Carl Simonton, a radiation therapist, and from Stephanie Matthews-Simonton, a psychotherapist. For the medical profession, they pioneered the exploration of psychological factors in the onset and treatment of cancer (Simonton, Simonton, & Creighton, 1978). Their fundamental question to a person facing cancer was, "What are the reasons why you want to die?" Along with this deep inquiry into the will to live or the will to die, they taught patients a system of relaxation and visual imagery, to be used three times a day. Patients and their spouses or other close "support" persons came to Texas for group therapy with Carl and Stephanie, repeated at intervals. Most patients continued medical treatment near their homes.

I had also done some work with Dr. Brugh Joy in relation to cancer. He, before meeting Dr. Simonton, had developed a method which he called Command Therapy, including relaxation and visual imagery. Its six steps were similar to those of the Simontons, but had some differences (Joy's Way, 1978). Like the Simontons, he saw the profound importance of the life and death issue. He helped patients to realize that the cancer, whatever else might be said of it, was providing a Big Change. If the individual were, consciously or unconsciously, seeking a major change in his life-pattern, the cancer would be consistent with this desire, even if the change were death of the physical body. Dr. Joy believed that a part of the person always knew intuitively that it was in some sense continuous and immortal, and that, therefore, from the standpoint of the "immortal self," death of the body from cancer could provide an acceptable answer to the person's wish for a big difference in the quality of life. It would be bringing about a great change from the current circumstances.

With this understanding of what might be the dynamics underlying the appearance of the disease, the person could look at his life and decide whether he could make a change which would make life worth living, or whether the choice would be to allow the disease to take its course and to bring the change in the form of death. If what the person was really sensing as necessary was a deep change, and if this were made in a sufficiently sweeping manner, the person would have no need of cancer and no need of death to bring that about. It would already have been made to the individual's satisfaction, and would have made life worth keeping.

The third facet of my preparation to do a specialized therapy with persons facing cancer was my understanding of the transformational process—to want one thing. During my contacts, first with the Simontons and later with Brugh Joy in working with cancer, I realized that for certain individuals at a particular point in their development, their "soul's growth," a life-threatening disease like cancer could provide the critical motivation for considering The Big Change, the wanting of one thing only, in an identification with wholeness. This desire to be open to express appropriately WHATEVER is called for from an inclusive perspective, is one which can be satisfied. The power to will this one thing lies within the individual and is not dependent upon anyone or anything for its fulfillment. Thus the choice to will this one thing is tantamount to having what one wants. It fulfills what one has desired, no matter what else may be going on, including cancer in the body. The choice is to open and allow the expression of wholeness . . . WHATEVER, or to be closed to that.

If something deep within a person is seeking a profound change which answers the need for a relationship with or a recognition of oneness with What Is, then the conscious choice to make this change meets that deeply felt urge, and the cancer is no longer needed for that purpose. Experience has indicated that under such conditions the disease process itself may be affected. However, the number of persons ready and willing to enact the shift to the single will is not large. In most instances, though not all, cancer patients choose to use some or all of the resources of medicine to deal with the disease when it presents itself. But, with or without medical intervention, the inner orientation of the person is of critical importance to the sense of well-being and enhanced quality of life.

All of these ideas were in my consciousness as I drove the four hundred miles to Hemet. Also I was thinking of a recent experience I had had in another country. A series of circumstances had led to my living for several weeks in the home of a woman whom I knew only slightly. She did not have cancer, but did have physical problems which seemed to me to be related to deep neurotic patterns which she kept repeating. It would have been impossible for me not to notice how she began to make some changes in her habitual responses, as the weeks passed and we engaged in all sorts of activities together, and discussed the meaning of "wanting one thing." Additionally, some parts of the experience were irritating to me, and I had ample occasions to explore acceptance and love . . . WHATEVER.

But it had been an experience of the unique opportunity which is afforded when two people can interact on multiple levels, with a shared interest in personal integration. Perhaps it encouraged me to believe in what might be the possibilities for the work which Gertrude Karnow and I were undertaking together. The motivation of crisis was present, and we both knew it. Something was needing to happen.

And we began to let it happen. We settled into a comfortable mixture of day-to-day activities—marketing, preparing food, sharing meals and conversation with Gertrude's husband Sidney, interacting with two little dachshunds, washing dishes, taking walks and sitting talking by the hour.

There was a minimum of structure to anything we did. There was a minimum of focus on the cancer, per se. Since the cancer, if that was what it was, was threatening her life, she did look long and deeply at why a part of her might be wanting to die. She saw that the refusal even to have a biopsy could be a form of denial that was serving a hitherto unrecognized will to die.

She asked herself, "Why might I be wanting to die? What in my life could possibly be so unfulfilling that I might choose to die? What in my life would I have to change in order to want to live? Am I willing to open to consider basic changes in my life, which might make life worth living? Could that possibly be worth the effort?" She began to search for the answers to these questions.

She looked at her life-long pattern of "mothering" others. She was the first child born to a young bride who was not really prepared to be a mother to this first baby or to three subsequent babies. When the second one was born, little Gertrude, aged two and a half, felt that she received the message, "Don't give us any trouble; take care of your little sister." And she had been faithfully following this general mothering path for some sixty-five years.

Her choice of work allowed her to express this mothering

with her clients whom she served devotedly. Her professional training and experience kept her "giving" within bounds, but left little or no place for viewing a total situation in which she too, had need for receiving and for nurture. She became aware of a rigid, compulsive pattern of work, according to a fixed programming for her life.

One very big and immediate problem concerned the relationship of some forty-seven years with her husband, Sidney, who had retired about three years previously, after an active and successful career as a salesman. Various changes in them both, and in their circumstances, had precipitated a series of crises involving intense pain to them both. They had tried a separation, had then re-established the relationship, and were again experiencing acutely distressing problems.

It was at this point that I did something I had not previously done in a therapeutic interaction. I shared very deeply and honestly with Gertrude some of my own experience with Bert, including the period of Tanya and the open marriage. This seemed clearly to open the way for a very honest, easy, mutually-appreciative free flow between us as we worked.

Whole new vistas of possibility emerged as we talked. Gertrude began to see how her well-organized, sometimes rigid ways were preventing any chance for real spontaneity, freshness, or newness in each life circumstance as it presented itself. Instead, without her awareness, she often obeyed an inner, rigid rule which decreed, "I am the sort of person who always . . . ," and her behavior was thus programmed without any chance for choice in each new moment.

Actually there were no completely "new moments" for her, due to the conditioning which limited her vision and actions. Also, because the habitual moments were increasingly felt to be unfulfilling and not worth the effort to go on, she was unconsciously beginning to give up the struggle.

She began to look at what would have to change in her life, and to ask whether she could even conceive of making certain big, drastic alterations. She became aware that some of her long-held ideas and habits of action were maintained unconsciously with a degree of rigidity which prevented fluidity and the opening to new options or different possibilities. She had assumed that many things were simply "not for her."

She found that she was afraid to consider certain of the most sweeping changes which might become necessary. This, in turn, helped her to enlarge her view and to consider whether, without answering the questions about specific actions, she might perhaps open herself to a larger, more general question, "Would I be willing to consider the possibility of allowing the emergence in my life of WHATEVER might be most inclusively appropriate, no matter what form that might take, and no matter what that might call for from me in the way of changes in my life? Could that kind of life be worth living?" There began to emerge for her a glimpse of a level of life she had not previously allowed herself to consider for herself, in which a kind of freedom and spontaneity looked new and appealing, perhaps waiting to be savored by her.

Slowly, very slowly, she began to find within herself the answer to the question, "Do I want to live or do I want to die?" But she had still not been able to say "Yes" to a biopsy.

The one essential thing I had to continue to do was to allow her to be where she was regarding the use of conventional medical treatment. Everyone else was pushing her to have a biopsy and to have surgery or whatever else was prescribed. I had moments of thinking that her path was an insane one and was very probably going to be fatal. However, I maintained my own center, and my inner state of willingness which made it possible to accept her wholeheartedly, with whatever decision she made. And of course, if her inner choice was to die, the path she was pursuing was eminently sane and would be effective.

When we discussed all of this later, Gertrude said that what had been determinative for her was that my attitude of acceptance of her right to make this life or death choice gave her all the freedom she needed. "If someone can have that faith in your being, in your process—that's really unconditional love. That leaves you wholly free to make your choice, and you don't do it for another human being, but because it's right for you to do. . . . So I saw that it was all right for me to make those choices. . . . That's a beautiful gift to give to another human being; I don't know anybody that ever said this to me before."

Out of all of these elements and many others, Gertrude slowly made the choice for life, with WHATEVER changes that would call for from her, and she scheduled the biopsy, nearly four months after she had found the lump. Sidney and I were with her and waited together during the next forty-five minutes. In that space of time, fully conscious, she experienced the skilled work of the surgeon and received the pathologist's report which she already "knew" would indicate a malignancy.

A few moments later Sidney and I heard her calmly and confidently discussing with the surgeon the fact that she would enter the hospital that afternoon and that he would perform the mastectomy the next day.

In the biopsy, everything seemed to come together, and her decision to have the surgery was wholehearted. As she described it later, "Everything said GO. That was the message, and I go along with the universe. It was unconditional."

She sailed through the surgery in a state of consciousness more heightened than any she had previously experienced. Her recovery from the surgery was excellent and she tolerated well and with good courage all of the difficult physical adjustments which followed.

This was four years ago. For me it has been a privilege and an inspiration to watch Gertrude progressively letting go and allowing her life to reconfigurate in WHATEVER way is indicated to her from a central place of intuitive knowing. She and Sidney are still exploring just what form their long and meaningful relationship needs to take, for them both, but for Gertrude the choices now can come from a steady, balanced center where she feels that she is "flowing along with the universe."

Her work with individuals has deepened, and she leads groups and does workshops in which participants find significant help.

She is now able to say, "I wouldn't trade anything for what the confrontation with cancer has done for me. I am no longer the person who had that experience; a transformation has taken place. I am myself, detached but very caring on a more loving basis than ever."

Gertrude Karnow and I agreed upon the unusual step of my giving this case example without the device of changing the names and disguising the details. We could do this primarily because she had earlier made the decision to share, on cassette tapes, the meaning for her of her life-threatening illness. "A Conversation about a Personal Experience with Cancer" and "Toward Transformation through Cancer" (see Bibliography) are two tapes which she and I made, and which can convey to some therapists and some cancer patients and their families a moving, personal record of the powerful force which was set in motion by the crisis of cancer.

CHAPTER 20

Helps Along the Way

I N A VERY real sense, "but one thing is needful." The transformational process is to want one thing; it is to fuse our wholeness with The Wholeness. I have tried to describe what I think that means.

However, I now include a brief mention of a number of areas for possible exploration along the way. Employed exclusively, rigidly, or dogmatically, as if in themselves they deserved a total devotion, they would be found to be limiting and contracting. Employed with looseness, lightness, and a sense of balance, they may contribute to the central task we choose to undertake for our own fulfillment.

Forming and Maintaining the Central Intention

All of the following suggestions are presented as possible means to help us form a single intention and maintain that state of centered willingness to express WHATEVER seems appropriate from the perspective of an inclusive, expanded consciousness. If we are consciously pursuing the transformational journey, this is and will remain the focus of our lives. It represents the state of BEING out of which all of our DOING in daily life proceeds spontaneously and effortlessly. Perhaps it is true to say that all of the other Helps which will be listed here are part of the one "effort" which is required, namely: to get to the willingness state of BEING, and to BE in it as much as possible. This involves an endless process of expanding, heightening, and deepening of consciousness, but always from the same central core.

Meditation

In the living task of working toward this end, most people find that the single most helpful means is some form of what may be called meditation or prayer or focusing or attending or attuning. Some use quiet times, long or short or both, scheduled or unscheduled, regular or irregular, formal or informal.

No matter what we may do of this kind, it is essential that we be clear about why we are doing it. In the transformational process, the purpose of meditation (whatever its form) is to experience the fusion of our wholeness with the wholeness. It is the recognition of the union of what we are with All That Is. The purpose is to realize our true identity, which is our oneness with the whole. The purpose is that a sense of separation and lack be replaced by a sense of union and fullness, as the totality expresses as us.

Meditation in this meaning of attunement, recognition of oneness, fusion with the whole, is for us food and drink. It is spiritual nourishment which sustains and renews our beingness. Thus the Source sustains our life, which is Its life.

One of the significant contributions of Eastern thought is its emphasis on the practice of meditation. Pervasively, in varied systems of thought, one finds instructions and images and practices to silence the mind. The means suggested are multiple, but the teachings which seem to me most usable by a Westerner are those which make the full circle, describing how the silent mind becomes a conscious reality for us in the market-place, on the street, and at work, not merely in an isolated solitude. It is an openness state, an empty space which is filled as soon as it is made ready.

Knowing Ourselves

All of these Helps Along the Way are means of knowing ourselves better. We learn increasingly to see and accept as our own the many facets of ourselves, and this opens to us the possibility of other options to choose from, in our living.

A uniquely valuable tool is the personal journal, which can be commenced in the simplest possible way by a beginner who writes honestly what he or she is experiencing. Very productive special methods of dialoguing with a journal are also available. One such is described by Ira Progoff in *At a Journal Workshop* (Progoff, 1975).

Watching ourselves in action and noting how we are centered or uncentered can tell us much about our habitual conditioned patterns of response. We learn what makes us *re*-act emotionally, "pushing our buttons," so that we act from the energy level of a specific attachment, rather than from the balanced, integrated energy level of the centered Self which wants one thing.

Vitally important insights can be derived from dreams. Our dreams are parts of us, waiting to tell us things we need to know about ourselves. Before going to sleep, we may invite a dream that will illuminate some question we are working on. And on awakening, it seems to be important to lie still and allow the dream memories to form themselves into our waking consciousness. For help in understanding what our dreams are showing us about ourselves, we can look to our own intuitive wisdom and that which we may find in books, lectures, and seminars. Dreams are the major source of self-knowledge in certain forms of psychotherapy.

Psychotherapy

Dr. Janette Rainwater, herself a highly skilled therapist, has written an unusually readable book called *You're in Charge!: A Guide to Becoming Your Own Therapist* (Rainwater, 1979). This is indeed the goal, for the client and for the conscientious therapist, but it is equally true that at certain times and under certain circumstances, we may make notable strides in our "soul-growth"—the consciousness of our wholeness—with the help of another person, professional or otherwise.

From the standpoint of the transformational process, it is obviously highly advantageous if the therapist we consult is also a person whose central orientation is that of wanting one thing, and of detachment from specifics. Such well-trained, experienced therapists with a basic orientation in what may be called transpersonal psychology, are becoming increasingly available in certain places. Their way of working is beautifully described by Dr. Frances Vaughan, a psychotherapist who has been in the creative forefront of transpersonal psychology as a recognizably distinct branch of psychology. In an article for the Journal of Transpersonal Psychology, she has described the distinctive elements of a psychotherapy which is carried on in a transpersonal context (Vaughan, 1979). Similar points of view are expressed in *Beyond Ego: Transpersonal Dimensions in Psychology,* edited by Roger Walsh and Frances Vaughan in 1980.

The willingness of increasing numbers of therapists to widen their views of what they themselves are, and to see how they may relate that to All That Is, inevitably allows them to see new possibilities for growth and expansion of consciousness in those with whom they work. One can sense that a transformational psychology is in the making.

In psychotherapy, no matter what form an individual's difficulties may take, and no matter how much time is consumed in working out particular problems or particular patterns that are causing trouble in the life of the person who comes for help, one inescapable fact remains. That fact is that, sooner or later, for the true resolution of any of the specific problems, no matter how extensive, the person must come face to face with one simple choice: to continue in essentially the same old way or to make the change from personal-self-direction to Undefined—WHATEVER-Is-Appropriate-Direction. Unless and until this happens, the same old struggle must go on, even though it may take other forms, even though the drama has a change of scene or of actors.

I am not downgrading psychotherapy as such. It can be extraordinarily useful as an adjunct. What I am upgrading is the transformational process itself, which goes beyond the level at which much psychotherapy ends. A psychotherapy based on the centered Self which wants one thing is a further step which fundamentally alters and integrates the personality structure, the Being, of an individual who takes that step.

Myths, Symbols, Fairy Tales

These represent a whole area of riches awaiting our exploration. For rational, linear-minded, left hemisphere-of-the-brain types, such as I have tended to be, they open doors to intuitive, wholeness-perceiving right hemisphere experience which may be otherwise inaccessible. They represent a portion of the collective consciousness of the race, a part of the wholeness with which our expanding awareness allows us to identify. The presentation of their immense possibilities for our growth is one of the striking contributions of the psychology of C.G. Jung and his followers. Astrology, the Tarot and the I Ching are forms of ancient wisdom which help some people to answer the question, "Who am I?" Like all of these Helps, they serve us best when we view them as means and not as ends in themselves.

Body Therapies

Many of us who get involved in exploring consciousness tend to neglect the fact that we are inhabiting a body which requires a lot of appreciation and use and tender, loving care. Physical exercise appropriate to our circumstances is basic. Relaxation of the whole body may do more than any other one thing to prepare us to engage fully in the transformational process. A significant element in relaxation and freedom from stress is right breathing which is taught in many body therapies as well as in meditative disciplines. Biofeedback and autogenic training have been helpful to many. Formalized movements such as T'ai Chi or the stretching postures of Yoga, or free-form expression in movement to music, or simply in spontaneous responsiveness, can enrich our lives.

A great many helpful body therapies exist, some of which can be done individually, and some of which require a helper, professional or otherwise. I found myself laughing as I wrote this and thought of sex as a body therapy, which in most but not all instances "requires a helper, professional or otherwise!" Sex is one of the important energies and capacities we possess as human beings. Its expression is similar to all the rest of our potentialities and energies in that the form, place, time, and manner of its expression may either proceed compulsively from the pressure of a specific desire or may flow from our integrated center which wants only to express WHATEVER is appropriate in the circumstances. The guidance, as in all things, comes from the single will to express WHATEVER represents wholeness for us, moment by moment, when we are willing to consider any possibility.

Nutrition

This deserves special emphasis for our well being, and receives it from a growing number of individuals and groups. Discrimination is needed to sort out the sometimes-conflicting views one meets, but the wisdom of an adequate, well-balanced intake of wholesome food is obvious. In the case of illness, and particularly certain illnesses, proper nutrition can be determinative.

One of the wonders which we tend to take for granted is the way in which our bodies constantly transmute into usable energy, the energy which we take into the body from other life-forms. It is another example of wholeness, of construction and destruction in an endless cycle of oneness.

Modern Science

In my own development along the transformational path in recent years, I found notable clarification and support from the current views of some scientists concerning the nature of reality. There exists now a literature in sub-atomic physics, microbiology and parapsychology which accords remarkably with the age-old wisdom of the mystics. One of my early contacts in the Parapsychology Research Group near Stanford University was with the American astronaut and Doctor of Science, Edgar D. Mitchell, and with two physicists, Harold E. Puthoff and Russell Targ of the Stanford Research Institute. The three had collaborated on carefully controlled research into capacities for clairvoyance, telepathy, and psychokinesis. Later, Puthoff and Targ published additional impressive findings on what they term "remote viewing" in their book entitled *Mind Reach* (Puthoff and Targ, 1977).

Meanwhile, Edgar Mitchell left the investigation of outer space and focused on the exploration of inner space, founding the Institute of Noetic Sciences, which continues in the forefront of the investigation of consciousness in many important human arenas.

These interests of mine took me to one of the first conferences in which the young Austrian physicist Fritjof Capra participated. His book, *The Tao of Physics* (Capra, 1975) was one of the earliest statements of the relationship between the findings of the most advanced sub-atomic physics and the essential ideas about the nature of reality to be found in the major Eastern systems of thought.

Currently, as I read of the scientific effort to formulate a Grand Unification Theory which can incorporate into one mathematical structure the forces that govern every event in the universe, I am inspired by what science and consciousness may accomplish together in expanding our understanding of What Is. We are able now to include the knowledge received not only from the areas which science has hitherto seen as the extent of reality, but also from the areas which are unquestionably available to consciousness and are increasingly being studied both in the laboratory and out of it.

Two strikingly impressive, encyclopedic volumes which describe such research are Marilyn Ferguson's *The Aquarian Conspiracy: Personal and Social Transformation in the 1980's* (Ferguson, 1980), and Barbara Brown's *Supermind: The Ultimate Energy* (Brown, 1980).

Illness as Teacher

Illness merits consideration as a possible help along the way although the issues it raises take us far and deep. What one comes to feel, on the transformational path, is that everything can be a teacher, including sickness of the body. Whatever else one may be doing in the way of treatment of a disease, the question is always present, "What is for me the personal meaning of this illness at this time?" The answer can be an important element in one's self-knowledge and can in some instances affect the course of the illness.

We know that the immediate tendency, in the face of illness in ourselves or others, is to make the value judgment that it is "bad" and is something to be resisted by every means available, and done away with as fast as possible. Another alternative presents itself as we move deeper into the idea of our own "wholeness." If we are an integral being which includes body, mind, and spirit, we may choose to ask what the disease may have to tell us. Our answer may determine what we choose to do about its presence in the body.

Illness is profoundly affected by our view of reality. The concept of wholeness as energy—fluid, flexible, in unceasing movement, and therefore changeable and mutable, rather than fixed and rigid, allows us to see disease in the body in a new light, from a different perspective. Such a view of the body can affect its functioning. An attitude of openness and fluidity to the free flow of energy at all levels —body, mind, and spirit—appears to be the key.

Experience as Teacher

Looking back over our life experiences can help the growth of an important feeling of trust, and increase a sense of some connectedness in things, so that we are not feeling separate and alone in a world that may have little meaning.

We know how it feels to look back at the experiences that we have thought were horrible and destructive and/or shameful and "the worst possible." But we can begin to see that they were essential to our growth, and that without them we could never have come to the place where we are now.

The trust comes as we begin to discern the outlines of a design in the totality which requires *all* of its parts, including a part for us and for other people we see around us who do not now seem as different or as separate as we first perceived them.

As we learn more about what we are, and embrace it all as part of our wholeness, we find ourselves, knowingly or unknowingly, proceeding on a spiritual journey. The wonder is that, as we continue to want one thing, we find within ourselves the resources for taking each next step. This capacity is within each one of us, and it functions for us.

Books

What can I say about this? Obviously I believe in their possible efficacy or I would not be doing what I can to convey clearly something which may be read and may be found helpful. Books stimulate and nourish me, but how can I begin to refer by name to very many of them? I have mentioned a few, but there are others which deserve to be pointed out in connection with the single will, and which have much to offer. The bibliography includes a listing of some of these. Always it is well to remember that the most useful books proceed out of individual experience. And they help most when we view them simply as helping us to trust our own unique individual experience.

After I had written this, I received a note in French from my friend Dr. Paul Tournier, expressing delight that I was writing an autobiography. He added, "C'est toujours le vécu qui touche." Yes, and this is why I have at long last tried to open my life honestly to you, since it is what has been lived and experienced that may reach from one heart to the heart of another person.

Creative Art Forms

Expression in almost any form of creativity can deepen and expand one's understanding of the meaning of the transformational process. Sometimes the result is a product beautiful by almost any standard. Frequently the product may have little excellence or beauty by narrow, conventional standards, but serves significantly to increase self-understanding and permit self-expression. This may be particularly true if the individual has the courage to undertake an art form which is totally new to him or her.

Color and sound represent new worlds to most of us, when carried into areas we have not yet explored but which some adventurous souls are investigating. Toning, chanting, and the use of mantras have proven useful over the millennia. Sound at high intensities can be a total experience which opens us into expanded states.

Poetry, prose, music, dancing, working with clay, wood-carving, weaving, acting, painting or WHATEVER—may serve to open new doors of creativity. We have the choice to let ourselves go.

Nature

It would probably be impossible to overestimate the richness which is added to a life spent in some close proximity to nature. A beautiful account of such an experience may be found in *The Findhorn Garden,* written by members of the Findhorn Community in Scotland (Findhorn, 1975). Its relevance to the transformational process is that the deep level of appreciation of nature which some members of the Community have experienced can expand our understanding of the existence within nature of an ultimately mutually-supportive wholeness.

Very recently a wealth of new light has been shed on our relations with the nature kingdoms by means of the publication of Dorothy Maclean's *To Hear the Angels Sing* (Maclean, 1980). I heartily recommend this extraordinarily human story of her experiences at Findhorn and in North America, as she explored the reunion of humans with the "creative essences or living creative principles within nature." Her communication with the essences of plants and trees taught her that "we can deal with all levels of our world in a truly creative, reciprocal way and, in joyous company, move to still more creative realms along with the brothers and sisters who make the totality of planetary life. . . . What matters is that we, the knowing, growing tip of Earth consciously act from our divine centers."

Humor and Laughter

I recall that at a relatively early age someone informed me that a sense of humor was really a sense of proportion or perspective. Since my father told a lot of jokes, I had a chance to test out that theory, and it was true. Now I can see the same principle at work in some Zen koans and Sufi stories.

What seems funny or ridiculous or outrageous is funny because it outrages our sensibility from one perspective, and makes us laugh. So laughter is excellent practice in shifting perspectives, or really in shifting levels of consciousness. Norman Cousins, in his book *The Anatomy of an Illness* (Cousins, 1979), has made an important contribution to our understanding of the function of laughter as one of the factors in his recovery from a serious illness which resisted conventional methods of treatment.

Ritual

Throughout human history, rituals of various kinds have had a significant place in many cultures. Interestingly, in our day, certain formalized religions in which ritual has been heavily emphasized are now lessening that emphasis or changing it to other forms. In contrast to that, other groups are creating new rituals to heighten and to express their inner states. Ritual, too, may be something to explore as part of the WHATEVER to which we are opening.

Relationships

From what I have said about Love . . . WHATEVER, it will be apparent that relationships take on new depth and meaning, out of the centered will. In particular, the form of a deep primary relationship changes. The partner can help by being a mirror of ourselves, reflecting back what we are, including our blocks and attachments. To the degree that we, through the transformational process, are being able to fulfill ourselves individually, we can relinquish the destructive and futile expectation that someone else will do that for us, and this frees us to accept from the relationship the wonders inherent in an unconditional love.

There is probably no way to describe the depth and height and richness which are possible in a relationship between those who progressively relinquish the sense of separateness and increasingly identify themselves as part of an all-inclusive wholeness which they share, which they serve, and in which they are merged.

Group Process

One of the most helpful single experiences can be a high energy group of people, all of whom are committed to the transformational journey. A number of beginnings are being made to explore the possibilities in such collectives.

Throughout the world, a few successful communities are emerging in which such groups of people live and work together. Other groups exist because the individuals who form them are in touch through what unites them, and meet from time to time.

In both instances, their basic inner orientation allows them to express in ways which are constructively effective beyond their immediate group.

Teachers and the Great Teachings

It would be strange to complete this work concerning the transformational process without a discussion of the contribution of the great religions of man, Eastern and Western. It is probably apparent that I have chosen not to approach these systematized teachings directly, despite their obvious importance.

Rather I am offering a psychological approach—to want one thing—as my understanding of what lies at the heart of all great religions. This essence is what Huston Smith has described as the "primordial tradition" in his book *Forgotten Truth* (Smith, 1976).

The essence is not always easy to find in an organized religion with a long history. The original inspiration for the great religions has flowed from individuals who embodied the single will, the centered willingness, the voluntary surrender to what was conceived of as the Source, The Wholeness, God—and who did this with a purity and luminosity which transformed some of those whom they touched, directly or indirectly.

It is not to be wondered at that centuries and millennia after the death of such a one, the Presence may still be felt by some as an active, living reality. We do not have to understand such a phenomenon to appreciate it. My own view is that their greatness is a consequence of their sense of oneness with The Source, as ours can be, in our unique way.

Contemporary teachers, too, can and do provide help for the transformational journey, both by their beingness and by the wisdom of their teaching. However, with them as with the historical figures, and as with the authors of "How To" books, the real value for us comes not from our reverence or worship of someone other than and different from ourselves. The real value comes as we discover the meaning of wholeness, of which they and we are individual expressions.

The transformational process is the attunement to or fusion with something undefined, limitless, conceived of as the ultimate Source of All That Is. In the end, the sense of that union is what one lives by; it is our true nourishment and the basis of our sense of well-being and equilibrium.

CHAPTER 21

What About the World?

Two of my closest friends, Jack and Elizabeth Martin, have a tiny stone farm-cottage in the French country-side, where much of this book has been created. This morning as I prepared to work on the book, I felt an unaccountable sadness. It was so real that a lump came in my throat and tears began to fall. I tried to explain to Lys that I didn't know how to say something important that was still unsaid in the book. We had just been listening to a radio newscast, presented as always at a racing pace which taxed our French beyond its present limits, but still left an impression of world-wide chaos, confusion, and human brutality and stupidity.

"How can I say in the book that I do see the kind of world we live in, that I am aware of the suffering and of the possibility of almost total annihilation of things as we know them?"

Lys replied, "Why don't you just say so, very personally? You have seen how it has been throughout human history and you see how it is now. The answer is the same. There's no resolution to the problems unless it comes from individuals who are centered and willing to take WHATEVER action expresses wholeness. Your entire book is saying what this transformational process is."

I know that this is true. The reason for writing the book was the deep conviction that, in an ultimate sense, a single realization of oneness is called for, out of which all of our specific actions flow. Unless and until we are in that centered state of willingness to express WHATEVER is most inclusive, whole, and therefore unconditionally loving, our actions in relation to other people and life forms at every level will be limited, unbalanced, and destructive in the moment. Perhaps the real hope at the planetary level is that our actions from the uncentered self are becoming so intolerable that we will be forced into a recognition of our interrelatedness. The specter of global disaster may provide a motivating force to make us demand an answer adequate to our mounting problems.

You know what I think that answer is. I have repeated it so many times that I may have worn you out with it. I guess what I am trying to say this morning is that to BE centered in the willingness state of consciousness results day by day in specific, concrete actions in the world. But the actions come from a unique, inclusive, non-rejecting level of consciousness and are therefore different in their effects from those that come from an uncentered state of attachment to or rejection of specifics which are partial and limited. The task is to identify with the whole, and then to act accordingly in all the specifics of daily life.

Somehow it cheers me up to recall that this same truth is to be found in the sayings of wise ones from ancient times. We are told that a student asked the Buddha, "What does the seeker do before Enlightenment?"

"He hews wood and carries water."
"And what does he do after Enlightenment?"
"He hews wood and carries water."

I think I have made it clear that we cannot say in advance exactly what our commitment to wholeness will cause us to do or not to do. Nor can we say specifically what is the appropriate action for anyone else. The appropriateness comes from the centered willingness state, which spontaneously issues in an action or non-action which fits each situation, viewed as inclusively as we are able to see.

From this level of consciousness, the intention is constantly translated into specific, concrete action on this plane of existence, moment by moment.

"Heaven" is thus grounded into "earth." What is most inclusively universal is expressed in and through the individual consciousness. Following the commitment, surrender, willing of one thing—the relationship of the individual to the totality is not that of being merged in the sense of being "lost" in a universal Something. Rather the relationship is that of an individual moving into and through the merging to be "found" again. The transcendence which is experienced in the state of oneness with the whole is immediately and continually grounded in action in this world. It is co-creation. We share wholeness; we serve wholeness; we are merged with wholeness.

In the beautifully illustrated book *Faces of Findhorn: Images of a Planetary Family* (Findhorn Community, 1980), David Spangler wrote:

> If there can arise a significant number of human beings who can draw directly upon the incredible resources of the super-sensible realms, then we have the capacity for transforming this planet.
>
> People say, "What can *I* do? I am just a single individual." You are either manufacturing darkness through your own inner states of anxiety and fear and separation,

or you are creating light and revelation through your abandonment of those past states and your attunement to new ones. The world offers us much to be pessimistic about, but that which is within us offers even greater material for creative optimism. . . .

World transformation is something that anyone can be involved in, anywhere. The New Age is too vast to be contained within a single structure, person or group. We need only to ask ourselves, "Am I being a way? Am I simply being a satellite in orbit around fixed ideas, or a new sun giving forth my own light of revelation? What am I doing to transform myself and my world?" As we confront these questions daily in our living we will be the revelation of the answers and the creators of a world made new.

CHAPTER 22

Aging . . . Who, Me?

W HILE I WAS working on the dissertation and on the
book before I knew it was going to become an autobiography, Naomi Emmerling asked to interview me in
depth. She was doing an M.A. thesis about optimal aging
(Emmerling, 1980) and she was looking into the factors
that might be important in people who appeared to enjoy a
basic sense of well-being in their later years. She was interested in whether such people found that they were continuing with their developmental tasks in another phase of a
cyclical development, or were in a more static state.

   In preparation for our day's discussion, she sent a long
questionnaire for me to be thinking about. Our hours of
conversation were recorded and transcribed, and I was
amazed to see how much had flowed out spontaneously
and naturally, both about my own life and about the transformational process. Here are a few fragments from our
hours together.

"What about aging?" she asked.

I laughed. "Aging seems like something that happens to other people." That is true. These years since age sixty have been so rich and full and inwardly rewarding that I cannot identify them with a word that has such a different connotation in our culture.

"How do you see this phase of your life as different from other phases of your life?"

"It seemed to me as I thought about this that the essence of the difference is that this is really for me—and this would all be since 1969—a turning inward, and giving much more attention to consciousness, and to my own spiritual growth. And then from that place moving out in expression."

"What do you sense is the purpose and meaning of this stage of your life?"

"It occurred to me this morning that you could just say it's to get it all together, for me and for the whole of which I am a part. It's a way of using all the experience that I've had to date to grow and be part of what I think of as the New Age. Another more specific thing would be to live—and to share the meaning of—the transformational process in human life." This has resulted in the decision to do the cancer work and the writing and speaking.

"What do you feel you can do because of your maturity and experience that someone else younger can't do?"

"I think there may be a kind of steadiness which can be in a person this age which wouldn't be there much before, a perspective. It's a kind of bringing the results of a life-experience together. It's admitting that one hasn't used that experience maturely and wisely all the time, but I think it's—I suppose it's the perspective and the experience and the steadiness that can come from that. Perspective is a very valuable thing. Sometimes I think it's the whole business. But it can be done at any age. It's like getting above the level of the problem, instead of trying to deal with the problem directly—or getting up to another level where the problem almost doesn't exist in the same way.

"I feel like such a fool to be saying something like that when I got caught myself so recently. (This interview was taking place a month after the Ph.D. oral examination.) But you see I didn't stay in that state. And of course I knew I couldn't live in that state of being wiped out. And I really knew, even when I was yelling my anger and hurt, that the other person wasn't responsible for the way I was feeling. *I'm* responsible for the way I feel. So I don't waste as much time getting lost as I used to. That's a real difference. I really do know where I have to be. I make the choice to be in or out of the centered willingness state."

"Are there turning points and patterns or threads in your life that you can distinguish?"

"The events and occurrences, outer and inner, that were turning points, do seem to form a pattern. They were the times when I would be getting involved and caught up with specifics—whether it was a person, a project, or possessions—and then something would happen that I would have to let them go. They would be taken away in some fashion. There would be things to overcome through suffering and apparent loss."

There was a great deal more to the interview, but this last question has been an excellent one for me to continue to ponder. From what I have told you, you can see how the pattern has repeated itself. A child with a deep and unrecognized non-acceptance of herself finds ways for her bright, bouncy nature to earn her the acceptance of her grammar school comrades. Then the near-fatal accident results in facial scarring which complicates her acceptance in the boy-girl situation at the high school dance. A fire destroys all the possessions she has accumulated to age sixteen. To gain wide acceptance, she does all that is necessary to become a college student leader on a national scale, whereupon she almost kills herself with overwork and has to drop out of college and fails to graduate.

In the journey around the world, twenty-one years of

settled ideas about customs, mores, morals, religion, plumbing, food, social "progress," and the mind-body relationship are shaken up to a point of no-return. She has to let go of her notion of the unquestioned superiority of all the ideas she has held.

After the luminous and centering experiences of the 1929 summer at Camp Minnesing, she establishes and then loses the relationships with her best friend and her fiancé—who marry.

The next object of attachment is her husband, Bert Horn. You have seen how she was apparently willing to pay any price in order to have and to hold the love and approbation of this one person. It was threatened for years. It was finally taken away with his death.

And in that same period, she lost her home and nearly all of her physical possessions and ended up earning her room and board in a nudist park as a short order cook!

All of this placed her in an ideal position to recognize what she had learned from experience. The Frances of to-day puts it this way. The fact is that my satisfaction does not come from getting or keeping particular things, people, or events that I want. My satisfaction comes when I am getting what I want. When I "want the one thing" it's in my power to have it. No matter how one conceives of the transformational process, in no matter what setting of re-ligion or what system of thought or what scaffold for view-ing reality, the core must be something which satisfies a deep urge for fulfillment and essential inner well-being.

From childhood on, we search for this "outside" of our-selves, and in specifics. We seek and grasp and try to hold on to things, people, and events, and we avoid, reject, re-fuse, and try to get away from other specific things, people, and events.

This is a hopeless process.

That is really all we need to see—that this way of trying to find satisfaction *cannot* work. There is no possible way that we can control all of the elements of a situation, including the feelings and actions of others, to suit our specific wants. Frustration is built into all such efforts, as is inner conflict (when our desires are self-contradictory), and as is a sense of being the victim of what people, things, and events are doing to us.

The alternative provides freedom from all of this. When the only thing I want is to be willing to express WHATEVER wholeness indicates as appropriate, I have what I want. I am identifying myself as part of What Is, inclusively, and I am fulfilled as I let that express as me. I am not attached to any particular form that may take. Thus, the solid foundation for my life is not disturbed when this or that specific occurrence takes place or fails to take place.

What has this to do with aging? Nothing unique. The principle is the same, no matter what our age. The specific problems which confront us at different ages may vary widely. But at any age there are but two ways to deal with them. We can choose to be open to express Wholeness or we can be closed, by attachment to specifics. Many young people and many in their middle years have learned this and have made the choice for Wholeness, with resultant joy, wholeheartedness, energy and love.

Many "aged" persons have learned it too, with the same results. They know that remaining at the problem level without the willingness state of consciousness is a dead end. No matter what is going on, no matter what has to be faced, any efforts merely to "cope" by means of the uncentered, attached self *cannot* give us the quality of life that we are all seeking.

Recently my attention has once again been drawn to the brilliant work of Dr. Hans Selye, in pointing out the part played by stress in many disease states. In discussing psychological factors in the causation of disease, he emphasizes the "destructive effect of unresolved contradictory efforts" and he affirms that "frustration and indecision are the most harmful psychogenic stressors" (Selye, 1978).

This perfectly describes why to want the one thing can result in a sense of well-being, even well-being of the physical body. To the degree that a person of young or middle years embraces this way of life, "the most harmful psychogenic stressors" will be absent from day to day living. In the same way an older person, facing whatever life brings, can do so without the strain and stress of unresolved contradictory efforts and without frustration and indecision. For any age group, this approach to life is wholehearted, from the core of the being. From the standpoint of quality of life, wholeheartedness and well-being are synonymous. Additionally, wholeheartedness is being found to have remarkable, perhaps almost limitless possibilities for the health of the body as well.

The choice to live wholeheartedly, wanting the one thing, is ours at any age. "Enlightenment is only a thought away." But a person of mature years may have a certain advantage by being able to look back at so many examples of the way that doesn't work. The perspective from this vantage point can provide an added stimulus toward the essential step into a free-flowing, flexible willingness state.

I am inspired by the sight of men and women of advanced years who are letting go of former fixed beliefs and behaviors and are recognizing their oneness with the Whole and are offering all that they are to the collective of which we are all a part. Their wisdom and experience can enrich us all. We do not know what circumstances the future may hold. We do know that there is a way to move into that future as beings who feel whole, free, and fulfilled.

CHAPTER 23

Identification . . . An Expanding
Awareness

THE TRANSFORMATIONAL PROCESS provides us with a
single, stabilizing, integrating center for all that we
are, WHATEVER that turns out to be as our awareness of
what we really are expands to include wider and wider
dimensions of reality. As a beginning, the collective which
we are includes every molecule of the physical body and
every intricate, complex connection and function among
all the parts of the body. All that we are includes the
natural pattern of a human body which exists and influences the manifested physical body. And we are more.

What we are includes the full range of our basic bio-
logical urges, our needs and desires, our emotions, feelings,
and moods. And we are more.

All that we are includes all of our senses, known and
unknown to us. It includes our perceiving abilities with the

187

senses we acknowledge. It also includes vast powers of intuitive knowing which we possess and which are ready to function for us and to provide direction as we acknowledge them as part of the wholeness, and allow them to express from our center in WHATEVER way is appropriate. And we are more.

We have rational capacities, seductive to a scientifically-oriented society but potentially dangerous until they are integrated into the balancing center of willingness to act from an expanded view of the whole. When they serve wholeness, our mental abilities help to illuminate our world. We are our intellects and we are more.

Above all, what we are is a capacity to choose, to will, to form intentions, purposes, directions for our lives. These are usually fragmentary, multiple, conflicting, and therefore often frustrated. But when this capacity to choose is focused and centered, attuned to WHATEVER wholeness may require of us, it moves us into a higher level of consciousness and opens us to possibilities of unlimited wisdom and power and love. This fusion of all that we are with All That Is is our spirituality. This recognition of the union of our wholeness with The Wholeness (WHATEVER that may be) allows the emergence of the centered Self, which knows that it is wholeness expressing. This comes about by the choice to want the one thing.

We set the intention in advance, in toto, and in general, to move with WHATEVER seems called for from us, in the direction of wholeness. All of the personality-level capacities and energies remain as potentials at their appropriate levels, but they are integrated by being at the disposal of WHATEVER response the total situation calls for. They rest at the direction of the centered will which wants one thing. The personality-level, ego-level energies and responses are not destroyed, wiped out, or repressed. They continue to exist as part of the limitless possibilities of response of the spirit, mind, emotions, and body, and are available to the integral Self which emerges at another level of consciousness by the choice to embrace WHATEVER represents wholeness.

We still have to choose which of all the options in a situation seems indicated for our response, but we have to be willing to do any of them. It is our single, generalized, prior commitment which guides us.

Two very important books deserve to be recommended here. *The Choice Is Always Ours* (Phillips, Ed., 1975) is a unique and invaluable anthology of the transformational process, presenting excerpts from many cultures, ancient to modern. *Man The Choicemaker* (Howes & Moon, 1973) was written by Elizabeth Boyden Howes and Sheila Moon, two of the founding leaders of the Guild for Psychological Studies. The Guild, with San Francisco and Four Springs headquarters, includes in its work Dr. Sharman's approach to the *Records of the Life of Jesus* (Sharman, 1917), and adds its insights from Jungian psychology.

As long as we are not at the inclusive level of awareness of what we are, but are in a narrower, more constricted personality-level of consciousness, we live with a sense of lack. We want more; we want something other; we feel that we haven't enough; that we are not enough; that we need to become more and to have more. Consciously or unconsciously, these feelings of vital lack gnaw at us unceasingly and wear us down physically, mentally, and spiritually.

This sense of lack derives from a sense of separation, of isolation. We feel separated from the source of supply. We are not in touch with anything capable of nourishing us completely. We are not full-filled. We feel lack, emptiness, separateness, and this acts to move us powerfully to seek fulfillment.

The greatest gift of the transformational process is that it fully nourishes us. It full-fills us. Our previous sense of lack has driven us to incessant wanting of specifics to fill the lack. When we voluntarily let these go, to embrace wholeness, we have returned to the Source.

This fusion transforms the quality of our lives. Out of it, from all the varied levels of our beingness and all the parts of ourselves, can flow WHATEVER response is appropriate in each moment. We learn that we are wholeness expressing, and so is everyone and everything else.

In this fusion, the centered Self recognizes and experiences the fact that it *already is* an integral part of the oneness that is existence, and that there is no "other" and no "outer" and no "inner." Identification with wholeness takes place. With this shift in perspective, the centered Self is BEING wholeness in unique, individual expression.

It is only the will that can achieve this. The physical nature alone, or the emotional or the mental, cannot achieve this merging into oneness. By means of the will we may voluntarily attune every possible aspect of our beingness into oneness with the whole. This is our spirituality, this choice to direct the personal collective that we are, into conscious attunement with The Collective, WHATEVER that may be, in its infinity. In this way, all that we are, in its multiplicity, is placed at the service of All That Is, and the two are seen and felt to be one. There is nothing that we have to *become*. We have only to recognize what we already *are*—inseparable parts of a whole, which excludes nothing and no one, as it includes everything and everyone. In the end, we each make the choice of how long to stay unaware of who we really are.

As I come to the end of this sharing of my life with you, I find two more bits of experience which I'd like to offer to you. Both are small glimpses of ways in which identification with wholeness may come to us. One is a gem from David Spangler's *Revelation: The Birth of a New Age* (Spangler, 1976). David faces me with the undeniable fact that a young American can be human, funny, and fully grounded in this physical dimension, while at the same time communicating simply and naturally with higher energies of spirit in other dimensions of life. While he was a co-director of the Findhorn Community in Scotland he received some communications of wisdom and counsel from a presence which identified itself as Limitless Love and Truth. The detailed counsel which was given to the Community by Limitless Love and Truth was summarized more than once in the simple words, "Be what I am. Live my life."

I have found these words profoundly moving. Sometimes when I am re-establishing my own central, single intention, I think of wholeness saying to me, "Be what I am. Live my life." And I reply to wholeness, "Be what I am. Live my life." In this inner conversation, Something is not directing something else. Wholeness is being itself, in outer, individual expression.

Another experience of oneness came as I just looked out of the window of this farmhouse in France where I am writing. The hill below me runs down to a small stream in the valley. The sight of a wind sweeping across a field of high grasses and wildflowers suddenly epitomizes for me the meaning of wholeness, the nature of the universe. That invisible stirring of the air is communicating itself one by one to each separate blade of grass, which in turn affects the one next to it until the whole hillside is in rippling, rhythmic movement.

That brings vividly to my awareness the hours I spent in an underwater observatory at the Great Barrier Reef off the coast of Australia, watching as the waves moved gently across an expanse of pink and violet sea anemones, each tentacle a couple of inches tall, waving in a graceful ballet, and each one responsive to the other and to every motion of the vast ocean in which it was immersed.

Such beauty is of the sort which "stabs one broad awake." I *feel* the movement of the wind and of the waves. I *am* the grasses and the sea anemones. I *know* that all is a oneness, all is wholeness in expression, and we are that.

I do not know what wholeness is. I cannot know and I need not know. It remains an undefined, infinite reality. But by now it seems clear to me that it is inclusive, rejecting nothing as "other," and expressing in unconditional love. My part is to allow this identification of myself with wholeness to be a living truth in my life by embracing it wholeheartedly and by letting go of everything that impedes its expression outward into the world. My willingness to entertain any possibility allows the emergence of the one that fits each situation, viewed as expansively and inclusively as my awareness permits. My willingness opens me to communicate with the creative forces in WHATEVER dimension they may be found.

"My wholeness, WHATEVER that may be, belongs to The Wholeness, WHATEVER that may be." This may sound abstract, and it is. But the abstractness is what allows for limitless expansion and flexibility. The abstractness is all-encompassing. It leaves room for me and for all of humanity to grow toward our infinite potential. But equally it is concrete, since it takes form moment by moment, in every action of my daily life, in relationships with other human beings and with all life forms.

WHATEVER I am belongs to The Wholeness, WHATEVER that may be. This affirms my universality and my individuality, simultaneously. I AM a focused center of wholeness; I AM wholeness expressing as me, and I allow it to be so, now.

As the realization of this grows in more and more of us, we are consciously co-creating the next step in evolution. We join with universal forces in a joyful celebration of our oneness.

Afterword

Now that I have completed this book, and have given you the insights from my life up to now, I will add a kind of glossary which may have some value for you. There is also a list of books. But, in the end, you and I both know that the only real value from the book can come as we experiment to discover whether The Way it describes can enrich and expand our own lives. Bon voyage!

Frances Horn
Carmel, California
May 1981

Definition of Terms

The Transformational Process—A way to personal integration. It is to want one thing; it is to choose to open and allow the expression of WHATEVER represents wholeness, moment by moment; it is to form and maintain one single, generalized, abstract desire, chosen in advance of and apart from specific situations—a single will to respond appropriately in WHATEVER way presents itself as most inclusive, expanded, and unconditionally loving.

The transformational process is the gradual shift from one inner state to another inner state—from a state of wanting to have many specific things, people, events in my life and refusing to allow many other specific things, people, events in my life—to a state of openness and *willingness* to allow WHATEVER response from my wholeness fits the situation as it is, viewed most inclusively, from my current state of awareness.

The transformational process, under whatever guise it appears in human history, always involves a wholeness in the individual which progressively identifies itself with the wholeness of What Is. It is the attunement to or fusion with something undefined, limitless, conceived of as the ultimate Source of All That Is. In the end, the sense of that union is what one lives by; it is our true nourishment and the basis of our well-being and equilibrium.

Want One Thing—The one thing I want is to say YES, in advance and in general, to WHATEVER may be appropriate in each moment. This means that I am *willing* to say *yes or no* to any specific possibility.

My single, generalized intention to respond appropriately in the moment frees me to try anything, to consider anything, because I am not hanging on either to a desire to do a particular thing, or to a "should," an "ought," a compulsion to go in a pre-determined way.

Instead, I am freed from numerous externally imposed moral standards because I have chosen a single, internally imposed standard, namely, WHATEVER is indicated to me as most inclusively appropriate in each unique situation, when I am willing to go in any way at all.

WHATEVER—A term that suggests the unlimited nature of my willingness to respond in a way which seems called for by the immediate moment, when the only thing I want is to allow that response.

WHATEVER does not label and does not exclude. It includes the opposites and the polarities. All options exist potentially in the WHATEVER.

WHATEVER indicates an open, undefined, unconditional potential in our wholeness and in The Wholeness of which we are part.

WHATEVER also suggests the unlimited nature of the universal processes we dimly discern but can increasingly see as inclusive of All That Is, excluding nothing and no one. In this sense, WHATEVER IS may be thought of as the Source, the reality out of which all forms appear and into which all forms disappear.

Wholeness—All That Is; the totality, WHATEVER that may be; the oneness which includes everything and everyone. I use the term in this universal sense, and also in the sense of my personal wholeness, which is part of The Wholeness and an expression of it. My personal wholeness, therefore, is inclusive of everything that I am, excluding nothing that I am. A result of the transformational process is my realization that there is no separation and that I AM Wholeness expressing uniquely as me.

Willingness—The inner state of openness to all possible options of response; it is a state of fluidity and flexibility toward all specifics. Such willingness is possible when I have chosen to want one thing—to allow the expression of WHATEVER may be the most inclusively appropriate response in each moment.

Willingness is the readiness to entertain any possibility in order to permit the emergence of what fits the circumstances, viewed from as wide a perspective as my expanding awareness allows. It is non-attachment to specifics, whether the attachment has been by desire or by aversion.

This willingness is a willingness . . . WHATEVER.

Appropriate—A centrally important term to describe my response to a situation. It is relative and changing, not fixed. My response is appropriate for me (not necessarily for anyone else) in this unique moment (not necessarily in another moment). Its appropriateness comes from my willingness to consider any response WHATEVER, in order to allow what fits the situation as I look at it from a level of consciousness which permits as wide a view as possible.

Knowledge of What Is Appropriate—A capacity which already exists in us as an intuitive knowing. We free it to speak clearly to us when the one thing we want is to hear what it is telling us, and to act accordingly. The limitlessness and inclusiveness of such available knowledge becomes more apparent as modern physics, transpersonal psychology, and ancient and modern mysticism, Eastern and Western, tell us more about the possible nature of energy/consciousness/Source/God. WHATEVER that may be, WE ARE IT, in unique, individual expression. Its wisdom is ours.

The condition for knowing what is appropriate is the intention, in general and in advance, to do WHATEVER is appropriate, when it is seen.

The Centered Self—The integration of all that I am, resting in a balanced, unified state of willingness and readiness to respond from WHATEVER level of myself—physical, emotional, mental, spiritual—is appropriate in each moment.

The centered Self is the unified Self which wants one thing, and which identifies itself with wholeness, WHATEVER that may call for in specific action or non-action.

Unconditional Love—The quality that expresses wholeness. It is the most characteristic response from the centered willingness state.

Unconditional love or limitless love or love . . . WHATEVER is not an emotion. It is a balanced, inclusive feeling-state which emanates from a view of the universe as one system in which everything is in relationship with everything else and inseparable from everything else. Unconditional love is, in fact, the realization that there is no "everything else" because all (WHATEVER that may be) is one.

The unconditional love which radiates from the centered Self is an expression of the appreciation we feel for life in WHATEVER form we find it, in ourselves and in others. As we are able to see the wholeness which already exists in us and in them, we open unlimited possibilities of expansion in us all.

Bibliography

A Course in Miracles. New York: Foundation for Inner Peace, 1975.

Anonymous. *The Impersonal Life.* Marina del Rey, CA: DeVorss & Company. (Originally published, 1941).

Assagioli, R. *Psychosynthesis.* New York: Penguin Books, 1976. (Originally published, 1965).

Assagioli, R. *The Act of Will.* New York: The Viking Press, 1973.

Bolen, J. Interview with Dr. Willis Harman. *New Realities,* June, 1978.

Bolen, J.S. *The Tao of Psychology: Synchronicity and the Self.* San Francisco: Harper & Row, 1979.

Brenner, P. *Health Is a Question of Balance.* Marina del Rey, CA: DeVorss & Company, 1980.

Brenner, P. *Life Is a Shared Creation*. Marina del Rey, CA: DeVorss & Company, 1981.

Brown, B.B. *Supermind: The Ultimate Energy*. New York: Harper & Row, 1980.

Burr, H.S. *Blueprint for Immortality: The Electric Patterns of Life*. London: Neville Spearman, 1972.

Capra, F. *The Tao of Physics: An Exploration of the Parallels between Modern Physics and Eastern Mysticism*. New York: Bantam Books, 1980. (Originally published, 1975).

Cousins, N. Mysterious Placebo: how mind helps medicine work. *Saturday Review,* October 1, 1977.

Cousins, N. *Anatomy of an Illness as Perceived by the Patient: Reflections on Healing and Regeneration*. New York: Norton, 1979.

D'Angelo, D. *Living with Angels*. Monterey, CA: Angel Press, 1980.

Deikman, A. *Personal Freedom: On Finding Your Way to the Real World*. New York: The Viking Press, 1976.

Dillaway, N. *Consent*. Unity Village, MO: Unity Books, 1947.

Dürckheim, K. *Hara*. London: George Allen & Unwin Ltd, 1962. (Originally published, 1956).

Dürckheim, K. *The Japanese Cult of Tranquillity*. New York: Samuel Weiser, 1974. (Originally published, 1960).

Dürckheim, K. *The Way of Transformation: Daily Life as Spiritual Exercise*. London: George Allen & Unwin Ltd, 1971. (Originally published, 1962).

Elixir. (Caddy, E.) *God Spoke to Me*. Forres, Scotland: Findhorn Publications, 1973.

Emmerling, N. *The Path of Optimal Aging: A Study of Self-Actualizing Older Adults.* Unpublished Master's thesis, Goddard College, 1980.

Ferguson, M. *The Aquarian Conspiracy: Personal and Social Transformation in the 1980's.* Los Angeles: J.P. Tarcher, 1980.

Findhorn Community. *The Findhorn Garden.* New York: Harper & Row, 1975.

Finegold, J., & Thetford, W.N. (Eds.). *Choose Once Again.* Foundation for Inner Peace. Millbrae, CA: Celestial Arts, 1981.

Golas, T. *The Lazy Man's Guide to Enlightenment.* Palo Alto, CA: The Seed Center, 1971.

Govinda, L.A. *Creative Meditation and Multi-Dimensional Consciousness.* Wheaton, IL: Theosophical Publishing House, 1976.

Greenwald, J.A. *Be the Person You Were Meant to Be.* New York: Simon & Schuster, 1973.

Grof, S. Theoretical and Empirical Basis of Transpersonal Psychology: observations from LSD research. *Journal of Transpersonal Psychology,* 1973, *1.*

Harman, W.W. The Excitement of Our Task: A Message from the President. *Institute of Noetic Sciences Newsletter,* Fall-Winter, 1978.

Hawken, P. *The Magic of Findhorn.* New York: Harper & Row, 1975.

Hine, V. *Last Letter to the Pebble People:* "Aldie Soars." Santa Cruz, CA: Unity Press, 1977.

Hixon, L. *Coming Home: The Experience of Enlightenment in Sacred Traditions.* New York: Anchor Press/Doubleday, 1978.

Horn, F. (Warnecke, F.D.) *A Psychological Study of the Dominance of a Generalized Desire over Specific Desires.* Unpublished Master's thesis, University of California at Berkeley, 1931.

Horn, F., & Karnow, G. *Toward Transformation Through Cancer.* Cassette tape, 1977. Southwest Audio, 216 East Broadway, Vista, CA 92083.

Horn, F. *The Process of Transformation.* Cassette tape, 1978. Southwest Audio, 216 East Broadway, Vista, CA 92083.

Hornaday, W.H.D., & Ware, H. *Your Aladdin's Lamp.* Los Angeles: Science of Mind Publications, 1979.

Howes, E.B., & Moon, S. *Man The Choicemaker.* Philadelphia: The Westminster Press, 1973.

Hubbard, B.M. *The Hunger of Eve: A Woman's Odyssey Toward the Future.* Harrisburg, PA: Stackpole Books, 1976.

Hubbard, B.M. *The Evolutionary Journal.* Washington, D.C.: Futures Network, 1978.

Huxley, A. *The Perennial Philosophy.* New York: Harper & Row, 1944.

James, W. *The Varieties of Religious Experience: A Study in Human Nature.* New York: Random House Modern Library, undated. (Originally published, 1902).

Jampolsky, G.G. *Love Is Letting Go of Fear.* Millbrae, CA: Celestial Arts, 1979.

Joy, W.B. *Joy's Way: A Map for the Transformational Journey. An Introduction to the Potentials for Healing with Body Energies.* Los Angeles: J.P. Tarcher, 1978.

Karnow, G., & Horn, F. *A Conversation about a Personal Experience with Cancer*. Cassette tape, 1977. Southwest Audio, 216 East Broadway, Vista, CA 92083.

Keyes, K., Jr. *Handbook to Higher Consciousness*. St. Mary, KY: Living Love Publications, 1972.

Keyes, K., Jr. *Prescriptions for Happiness*. St. Mary, KY: Living Love Publications, 1981.

Kierkegaard, S. *Purity of Heart Is to Will One Thing*. (D. Steere trans.). New York: Harper Torchbooks, 1956.

Latner, J. *The Gestalt Therapy Book*. New York: The Julian Press, 1973.

Lawrence, B. *The Practice of the Presence of God: Being Conversations and Letters of Brother Lawrence*. London: H.R. Allenson Ltd, undated.

Leonard, G. *The Silent Pulse: A Search for the Perfect Rhythm that Exists in Each of Us*. New York: E.P. Dutton, 1978.

LeShan, L. *The Medium, the Mystic, and the Physicist: Toward a General Theory of the Paranormal*. New York: Ballantine Books, 1966.

LeShan, L. *You Can Fight for Your Life: Emotional Factors in the Causation of Cancer*. New York: M. Evans, 1977.

Loomis, E.G., & Paulson, S. *Healing for Everyone: Medicine of the Whole Person*. Marina del Rey, CA: DeVorss, 1979.

Luce, G.G. *Your Second Life. Vitality and Growth in Maturity and Later Years from the Experiences of the Sage Project*. New York: Delacorte Press/Seymour Lawrence, 1979.

Maclean, D. *To Hear the Angels Sing: An Odyssey of Co-creation with the Devic Kingdom.* Elgin, IL: The Lorian Press, 1980.

Marshall, G.N. *Buddha: The Quest for Serenity.* New York: Beacon Press, 1979.

Merrell-Wolff, F. *Pathways Through to Space: A Personal Record of Transformation in Consciousness.* New York: The Julian Press, 1973.

Merrell-Wolff, F. *The Philosophy of Consciousness Without an Object: Reflections on the Nature of Transcendental Consciousness.* New York: The Julian Press, 1973.

Mitchell, E.D., & White, J. (Eds.). *Psychic Exploration: A Challenge for Science.* New York: G.P. Putnam's Sons, 1974.

Oyle, I. *The Healing Mind.* Millbrae, CA: Celestial Arts, 1975.

Oyle, I. *The New American Medicine Show.* Santa Cruz, CA: Unity Press, 1979.

Phillips, D.B., Howes, E.B., & Nixon, L.N. (Eds.). *The Choice Is Always Ours.* Wheaton, IL: RE—QUEST Books, The Theosophical Publishing House, 1975. (Originally published, 1948).

Pike, D.K. *My Journey into Self, Phase One.* San Diego, CA: LP Publications, 1979.

Plato. The Apology and the Crito. In Charles W. Eliot (Ed.), *The Harvard Classics.* New York: P.F. Collier, 1937.

Progoff, I. *At a Journal Workshop.* New York: Dialogue House, 1975.

Puthoff, H., & Targ, R. *Mind Reach*. New York: Delacorte, 1977.

Rainwater, J. *You're in Charge!: A Guide to Becoming Your Own Therapist*. Los Angeles: Guild of Tutors Press, 1979.

Rathbun, H. *Creative Initiative: Guide to Fulfillment*. Palo Alto, CA: Creative Initiative Foundation, 1976.

Satprem. *Sri Aurobindo or The Adventure of Consciousness*. New York: Harper & Row, 1968.

Selye, H. *The Stress of Life*. New York: McGraw-Hill, 1956.

Sharman, H.B. *Records of the Life of Jesus*. New York: Harper & Brothers, 1917.

Sharman, H.B. *Jesus as Teacher*. New York: Harper & Brothers, 1935.

Shealy, C.N. *90 Days to Self-Health*. New York: Bantam Books, 1978.

Shealy, C.N. & Shealy, M.C. *To Parent or Not: A Comprehensive Approach to Family Health*. Virginia Beach, VA: The Donning Company, 1981.

Simonton, O.C., Simonton, S.M.-, & Creighton, J. *Getting Well Again: A Step-by-Step, Self-Help Guide to Overcoming Cancer for Patients and their Families*. Los Angeles: J.P. Tarcher, 1978.

Smith, H. *The Religions of Man*. New York: Harper & Row, 1958.

Smith, H. *Forgotten Truth: The Primordial Tradition*. New York: Harper & Row, 1976.

Spangler, D. *Revelation: The Birth of a New Age*. Forres, Scotland: Findhorn Publications, 1976.

Spangler, D. *The Laws of Manifestation*. Forres, Scotland: Findhorn Publications, 1975.

Steiner, R. *Theosophy: An Introduction to the Supersensible Knowledge of the World and the Destination of Man*. New York: Anthroposophic Press, 1971. (Originally published, 1911).

Swaim, L.T. *Arthritis, Medicine and the Spiritual Laws: The Power Beyond Science*. Philadelphia: Chilton Company, 1962.

Swearingen, R. *Personal Evolution or The Yellow Brick Road Revisited*. Unpublished manuscript, 1978.

Tarthang Tulku. *Gesture of Balance: A Guide to Awareness, Self-Healing, and Meditation*. Emeryville, CA: Dharma Publishing, 1977.

Tarthang, Tulku. *Time, Space, and Knowledge: A New Vision of Reality*. Emeryville, CA: Dharma Publishing, 1977.

Tarthang Tulku. *Skillful Means*. Emeryville, CA: Dharma Publishing, 1978.

Tournier, P. *The Meaning of Persons*. New York: Harper & Row, 1957.

Tournier, P. *The Healing of Persons*. New York: Harper & Row, 1965.

Tournier, P. *Learn to Grow Old*. New York: Harper & Row, 1972.

Trine, R.W. *In Tune with the Infinite*. London: G. Bell and Sons, Ltd, 1965. (Originally published, 1897).

Vaughan, F.E. *Awakening Intuition*. Garden City, NY: Anchor Press/Doubleday, 1979.

Vaughan, F. Transpersonal psychotherapy: context, content and process. *The Journal of Transpersonal Psychology,* 1979, *2.*

Walsh, R.N., & Vaughan, F. (Eds.). *Beyond Ego: Transpersonal Dimensions of Psychology.* Los Angeles: J.P. Tarcher, 1980.

Wapnick, K. *Christian Psychology in "A Course in Miracles."* New York: Coleman Graphics, 1978.

Wieman, H.N. *The Issues of Life.* Quoted in the anthology *The Choice Is Always Ours.* Phillips, D.B., Howes, E.B., & Nixon, L.N. (Eds.). Wheaton, IL: RE—QUEST Books, The Theosophical Publishing House, 1975. (Originally published, 1948).

WHO AM I?

Photograph by Leah Williams Washington

"A short-order cook in a nudist park and a dinner guest in the palace of the Maharajah of Mysore." With these words Frances Horn begins her absorbing story. It conveys clearly and simply the universal Wisdom gleaned from a full and varied life. With honesty and openness, she shares a way to fulfilling our highest potential.

Frances Horn, Ph.D., is a psychotherapist whose academic background includes a B.A. and M.A. in psychology, M.S.W. in psychiatric social work, and Ph.D. in counseling psychology. Her most recent psychotherapeutic work has been with cancer patients. She lives in California, and travels extensively for lectures and workshops.

●

Frances Horn's warmth, humor and compassion accompanied by profound personal insights make this book an unforgettable experience for the reader.

—William N. Thetford, Ph.D.   Foundation for Inner Peace. Co-editor of *Choose Once Again.*

If she is willing to be that honest and to make herself that vulnerable to tell me what this Wisdom is, she must care about me.

—Dianne Roveto.   Wife, mother, teacher, person.

Frances Horn is a beautiful person who radiates her love throughout every page of *I Want One Thing.* She puts into practice the statement from *A Course in Miracles,* "Teach only love, for that is what you are."

—Gerald G. Jampolsky, M.D.   The Center for Attitudinal Healing. Author of *Love Is Letting Go of Fear.*

I WANT ONE THING by Frances Horn is a moving account of a transformational journey that spans a lifetime. In focusing on the central question, "Am I totally willing to do, feel, be WHATEVER is wanting to express as my whole self?" the author challenges each of us to respond from the depth of our being and reflect on our own willingness to commit to truth at any age, in any circumstances of life.

> —Frances E. Vaughan, Ph.D.   Past president, Association for Transpersonal Psychology. Author of *Awakening Intuition*. Co-editor of *Beyond Ego*.

Frances Horn's book is a study in honesty and perseverance. It is the story of a dream that took over seventy years to awake into.

> —Paul Brenner, M.D.   Author of *Health Is a Question of Balance* and *Life Is a Shared Creation*.

It will help people to read your story. . . . Because it is not an overwhelming revelation, it feels more as if it could be my own story too . . . and I can imagine myself proceeding, as you did, from a single-minded precept into my own transformation.

> —Gay Gaer Luce, Ph.D.   Author of *Your Second Life* and *Body Time*.

If each of us could be so clear in understanding our transformational journey, our positive evolution would be greatly enhanced.

> —Robert L. Swearingen, M.D.   Instructor in Orthopaedic Surgery and Preventive Medicine.

I love a person who can say, "At age 72, I had an experience that changed my life!" Frances Horn's autobiography . . . is an open, frank, refreshing self-realization that invites the reader to find the same secret for zest in living that the author has found.

> —Willis W. Harman, Ph.D.   Stanford professor of engineering-economic systems. President, Institute of Noetic Sciences.

Frances Horn, indomitable spiritual adventurer, has written a highly personal, insightful book. . . . It is a Horatio Alger story on attaining psychological and spiritual enrichment.

> —Jean Bolen, M.D.   Author of *The Tao of Psychology*.